T0113886

The Holydays of God, in Christ Jesus of Nazareth, with His Holy Spirit

DARRELL MOWAT

WESTBOW
PRESS*
A DIVISION OF THOMAS NELSON
& ZONDERVAN

WestBow Press books may be ordered through booksellers or by contacting:

WestBow Press
A Division of Thomas Nelson & Zondervan
1663 Liberty Drive
Bloomington, IN 47403
www.westbowpress.com
844-714-3454

All scripture quotations are taken from the King James Version.

ISBN: 978-1-6642-7598-0 (sc)
ISBN: 978-1-6642-7597-3 (e)

Print information available on the last page.

WestBow Press rev. date: 08/18/2022

Contents

Preface

This book came into being, from a few years of "wrestling" with Biblical doctrines versus Church tradition. Early on in my calling as a young man, I attended a church denomination that was somewhat different than the protestant church denomination, I attended as a child. They congregate on Saturdays, calling it the Sabbath and the seventh day of the week, and called themselves the "Church of God", with their specific denomination's prefix, the "Restored". I learned quite a few things about church history and the roots in Judaism of Christianity from this denomination, and they also taught the Old Testament from a Christ follower's perspective. The other gift the Church of God has, is of prophecy, albeit, prophecy is not the end all be all of life; it can be used as a warning and a blessing of hope (1 Cor. 13:2, 14:3, 4). The simple prophecy that Jesus Christ of Nazareth said of Himself and us, "...I go and prepare a place for you, I will come again, and receive you unto myself...", is probably the best prophecy I could possibly think of, outside of the Old Testament prophecies of Jesus Christ of Nazareth, as the Messiah, our Saviour (John 14:3). That all being said, one of the other differences that this denomination had, from "mainstream" Christianity, was that they keep the Leviticus 23 Holy days; putting them into proper perspective from a Messianic, point of view. Just like Jesus and the apostles also kept them, along with the Jewish and Israelite population of Jerusalem at the time, in the early first century A.D. (Matt. 26:17-19, John 7, Acts 2:1-4). This brings us to the purpose of and how this book came about; it is a book about these Leviticus 23 Holy days, focusing on the New Testament and Old Testament purposes of keeping them, and the "prophetic" message they tell in observing them (Ps. 19:11, Col. 2:17). With all that being said, let me go into, a little further, the "bigger picture" of the individuality we all have in our relationship with Jesus Christ of Nazareth, regardless of our religious background or denominational upbringing. Alleluia and praise the LORD. Amen and Amen.

Ezekiel 20 goes into detail about God's issue with Israel and the keeping of the Sabbaths and Holy days, and is also prophetic in things to come. God spoke to Isaiah and said, "Bring no more vain oblations; incense is an abomination unto me; the new moons and sabbaths, the calling of assemblies, I cannot away with; it is iniquity, even the solemn meeting. Your new moons and your appointed feasts my soul hateth: they are a trouble unto me; I am weary to bear them." (Isa. 1:13, 14). It has been suggested, that this is referencing foreign, unbiblical, feast days and so called sabbaths (Jud. 18, 1 Kings 12:32, 33; Ps. 119:126). However, we need to remember regardless of an "holy day" or "sabbath", that God, in Jesus Christ of Nazareth, is calling us to repentance and submission to Him by the forgiveness of our sins (Isa. 1:16-20). It is only by Jesus Christ of Nazareth's eternal offering on the cross at the holy day of Passover in 31 A.D., that we can receive eternal life. Jesus was conceived by the Holy Spirit in and born of the virgin, Mary, espoused to Joseph (Matt. 1:18-25). He was raised, a child of Israel, of the tribe of Judah, with brothers and sisters (Matt. 13:55, 56; Luke 2:41-52, Rev. 5:5). He began His earthly ministry at about the age of thirty in 27 A.D., and for three and a half years; He taught, forgave, and did other miracles (Luke 3:23). And at Passover in 31 A.D., He was crucified and died on the cross, shedding His Holy and righteous blood on the cross for the forgiveness of our sins. He was buried and the third day He arose to give us the hope and promise of eternal life in His Holy name. As Jesus said, "…Repent: for the kingdom of heaven is at hand." (Matt. 4:17). Alleluia and praise the LORD. Amen and Amen.

Why do people not know about the Leviticus 23 holy days? In the Lamentations of Jeremiah it says of God, "And he hath violently taken away his tabernacle, as *if it were of* a garden: he hath destroyed his places of the assembly: the LORD hath caused the solemn feasts and sabbaths to be forgotten in Zion, and hath despised in the indignation of his anger the king and the priest." (Lam. 2:6). It was because of our ancestors' rebellion, of the tribes of Israel, that the memory and knowledge of these feast days have been removed from our minds (Ezek. 20). At least as far as the "…lost sheep of the house of Israel…" are concerned, namely the Judeo-Christian people of western civilization; albeit there are, no doubt, descendants of the tribes of Israel throughout the whole world (Matt. 10:6). Just as if we disobey a simple command from our parents and go after our own ways, the memory of that way is removed from us (Ex. 20:12). It is the same with God, until we repent and turn to God in Jesus Christ of Nazareth, through the forgiveness of our sins, like the prodigal son, Jesus spoke of (Luke 15:11-32). That all being said, in the New Testament, Jesus simplified things for the "…lost sheep of the house of Israel…", and the whole world for that matter; by believing on Him, we have eternal life in His Holy name (John 3:16). Romans 14:5 says, "One man esteemeth one day above another: another esteemeth every day *alike*. Let every man be fully persuaded in his own mind.". Colossians 2:16 says, "Let no man therefore judge you…in respect of an holyday, or of the new moon, or of the sabbath days…". And Philippians 4:4 says, "Rejoice in the Lord alway…". The Old Testament prophet, Daniel, prophesied of those whom would, "…think to change times and laws…" (Dan. 7:25). The apostle, Paul, said of the Jews, whom kept the law of God; "What advantage then hath the Jew? or what profit *is there* of circumcision? Much every way: chiefly, because that unto them were committed the oracles of God." (Rom. 3:1, 2). This is the key to this book; the greater understanding of God's plan for mankind rests in obedience to God and His commandments (Matt. 19:17, 1 John 2:3). Jesus Christ of Nazareth confirms this, "…salvation is of the Jews." (John 4:22). Alleluia and praise the LORD. Amen and Amen.

Mainstream Church Calendar versus Biblical Holy days; with the former being said, let's take a closer look at the history of these holy days and the popular traditions that surround them since Christ's resurrection and ascension to the Father in heaven in spring of 31 A.D.. The message of salvation from the "mainstream" Church calendar, as of the date of writing this book in 2019 A.D., leaves out details of the full plan of God, it is more general, in some respects. That is; the commonly celebrated Christmas, Easter, Pentecost, Thanksgiving, and Halloween versus Leviticus 23 Holy Days, as of the date of writing this book in 2019 A.D.. The Old Testament Holy days, if kept and understood correctly, relay God's full salvation plan for mankind here on earth and into eternity, especially when putting them into the New Testament perspective of Jesus Christ of Nazareth, as the Messiah and the High Priest of these Holy days (John 5:39). This all being said there is unity through diversity in the name of Jesus Christ of Nazareth (1 Cor. 12:4-6). As mentioned earlier, we as Christ followers, Jewish or Gentile, are not to judge one another or cause a stumbling block to our brothers and sisters (Rom. 14:13). As the Bible says, "…*one* star differeth from *another* star in glory." (1 Cor. 15:41). God created us all individually, in Christ, and that is what makes this life so bright, exciting and hopeful; because we truly do not know all that God has done, is doing, or will do, for us as individuals or as the Body of Christ, as a whole. There is a sense of beauty and joy in variety, whether it is in nature itself, in cultures, or in religion, the most important thing is that Truth prevails. Jesus came in grace and truth after all (John 1:14). So with that all being said, if you are interested in learning more about the "Holy days" of God in the light of the New Testament Prophet, Messiah and Saviour, Jesus Christ of Nazareth, along with the Old Testament history, as well as in Biblical prophecies in general, read on. Alleluia and praise the LORD. Amen and Amen.

Acknowledgements

This book is written for the glory of God, and His only begotten Son, Jesus Christ of Nazareth, with His Holy Spirit; and for all those whom desire to seek and find the truth of God. Alleluia and praise the LORD. Amen and Amen.

Introduction

In this book, I will speak about God's salvation plan for mankind, put forth through the knowledge of and observance of His Holy days. The majority of which are mentioned in Leviticus 23. Using New Testament scriptures, I will show you that both Jesus and His disciples kept these days, as they were mostly of Jewish descent from the start; but more importantly, that as Jesus said, "…salvation is of the Jews." (John 4:22). Speaking namely about Himself, being the Saviour of the whole world, and Messiah, the Christ, of His kingly descent from King David, and in general from the tribe of Judah; but also, that the commandments God gave, of the Old Testament, have not been "done away with", completely. It is these commands of God that give us life, with a firm foundation in the knowledge of and acceptance of Jesus Christ of Nazareth, as the Saviour of the whole world, first and foremost. As Jesus said of Himself, "Think not that I am come to destroy the law, or the prophets: I am not come to destroy, but to fulfil." (Matt. 5:17). It is through Jesus Christ of Nazareth, that we have eternal life; do not be mistaken about that. But with this knowledge and greater understanding of God's salvation plan through the signs in the Holy Days; we can have a better understanding of the "greater detail" of God's salvation plan. I speak of, namely, prophesy and the knowledge of things to come in this world, and ultimately in "the world to come." (Col. 2:17). With that all being said, take time to read through the chapters of this book. In the end, the gospel message is simple, Jesus made it simple. As He said in John 3:16, "For God so loved the world, that he gave his only begotten Son, that whosoever believeth in him should not perish, but have everlasting life." (John 3:16). Alleluia and praise the LORD. Amen and Amen.

So in this book, I will touch on the solar and lunar calendars that are used today for keeping days, months, seasons and years. And then, I will go into the details of the Holy days, that are kept by the lunar calendar; which are as the Bible says, "…a shadow of things to come…" (Col. 2:17). Although much of the signs of these Holy days have been fulfilled, including Passover and the Days of Unleavened bread, and partially Pentecost, in the life of Jesus Christ of Nazareth; we await the final fulfillment of the purpose and signs of the fall feast days: the Feast of Trumpets, the Day of Atonement and the Feast of Tabernacles, including the Last Great Day (Lev. 23). It is in all of these days, that we see the message of salvation in Jesus Christ of Nazareth at Passover in 31 A.D., the outpouring of the Holy Spirit in Pentecost in 31 A.D.; and then at some point in time to come, the "Great Tribulation", the "Messianic Age", and last, the final day of Judgement with the "…new heavens and a new earth…", and the new Jerusalem, shown in the Feast of Trumpets, the Day of Atonement, and the Feast of Tabernacles with the Last Great day, respectively; as of the date of writing this book in 2019 A.D. (Lev. 23, Rev. 21:1, 2). This may seem like a lot of information, but the remainder of the chapters of this book, explain in greater detail, each Holy day and its purpose, in the Old Testament time, today and prophetically into the future. And how Jesus Christ of Nazareth's life here on earth, has fulfilled and been involved in all of these Holy Days of Leviticus 23. Alleluia and praise the LORD. Amen and Amen.

First, I will speak about the beginning, regarding God's creation history, with the sun and the moon, and then I will go on to talk about the seventh day God created for rest and sanctified to be Holy (Gen. 1:14-19, 2:2, 3). This simple, seventh day of rest, is the key to understanding the "bigger" picture of God's ultimate salvation message; as there is a 7000 year plan, God has for the inhabitants of this present earth's history, before the final resurrection and judgement (Rev. 20:11-15). This is the key to understanding where we are in human history, and understanding the "greater" plan God has for earth and mankind, in general. That is there is a 1000 year period of rest and peace, that has not yet taken place, as of the date of writing this book in 2019 A.D., some refer to as the "Messianic age", as mentioned earlier (Rev. 20:4, 6). As the Bible says, 1000 years can be like a day for God, so it is in this seventh day, the last 1000 years of God's salvation plan for mankind here on earth, that the earth and all whom inhabit it will receive a rest, and peace, from all sorts of evil that it has endured, the last approximately 6000 years that mankind has been "working" out our salvation, so to speak (Ps. 90:4, Phil. 2:12, 2 Pet. 3:8, Rev. 20:4, 6). God has given us the opportunity to subdue the earth, "rule" it, and have "…dominion…" over it (Gen. 1:28). Mankind has done many things throughout this time; our ancestors, Adam and Eve, fell in the Garden of Eden and the land was cursed, then the flood came, and the curse was taken from the land, after this God chose Abraham and his seed to continue His salvation message to this fallen world (Gen. 3, 6, 7, 17:9). It is through Isaac, Jacob, renamed Israel, then Judah, then King David of Judah, and other Old Testament prophets and then Jesus Christ of Nazareth, a descendant of King David, and His chosen disciples that this message would and does continue unto today (Matt. 1, 28:18-20). So keep this in mind when reading through the chapters and appendices of this book, putting the subjects spoken of into proper perspective, a godly perspective, in the name of Jesus Christ of Nazareth, God, the Father's, only begotten Son, through His Holy Spirit teaching you, in you and with you (John 14:16-18). Alleluia and praise the LORD. Amen and Amen.

CHAPTER 1

In the beginning

"And God said, Let there be lights in the firmament of the heaven to divide the day from the night; and let them be for signs, and for seasons, and for days and years:…"
- Genesis 1:14

Introduction

The two great lights; Genesis 1:15-19 continues and says, "And let them be for lights in the firmament of the heaven to give light upon the earth: and it was so. And God made two great lights; the greater light to rule the day, and the lesser light to rule the night: *he made* the stars also. And God set them in the firmament of the heaven to give light upon the earth, And to rule over the day and over the night, and to divide the light from the darkness: and God saw that *it was* good. And the evening and the morning were the fourth day.". This chapter is an introduction to the differences of how time is kept in this world. It includes the revelation of the truth and use of the "lunar" calendar as a "sign" and "shadow" of the greater plans of God, the Father, Almighty here on earth and in eternity also. In Isaiah 30:26, it says, "Moreover the light of the moon shall be as the light of the sun, and the light of the sun shall be sevenfold, as the light of seven days, in the day that the LORD bindeth up the breach of his people, and healeth the stroke of their wound.". This prophetic word given to Isaiah by God, will be spoken of from a few perspectives regarding the solar calendar, lunar calendar, and how these things are all related to Jesus Christ of Nazareth, the Saviour of the whole world, and our relationship with Jesus and God, the Father, and with His creation through His Holy Spirit, the Holy Ghost; past, present, future, and forever more in the "world to come". Alleluia and praise the LORD. Amen and Amen. Read on to learn more.

Greater

Genesis 1:16 says, "And God made two great lights; the greater light to rule the day…". Jesus Christ of Nazareth calls us to walk in the light, and says there is twelve hours in the day, so this should be a good indication of approximately how much time ought to be given to our daytime life (John 11:9). The Bible does suggest the righteous will shine like the stars, and Jesus Christ of Nazareth is referred to as the "…morning star…", in the book of Revelation (Dan. 12:3, Rev. 22:16). Also, Jesus Christ of Nazareth, at His transfiguration was referred to as having His face shine like the sun (Matt. 17:2). In reference to the solar calendar; the Julian calendar, originated around 46 B.C., by Julius Caesar, and adjustments were made, including adding August for Augustus Caesar.[1] There was a transformation to the Gregorian calendar in the second millennia A.D. and the Gregorian calendar has thirty-one day months and thirty day months.[2] The solar calendar also includes the solstices and equinoxes, which help indicate the seasons of the solar year; spring, summer, fall and winter. The winter solstice is when the sun shines for the least amount of time during the day in a year, and the summer solstice is when the sun shines for the most amount of time during the day in a year, using the northern hemisphere as a reference point. The spring and fall equinox are indicators of the equal amount of time the sun, during the day, and the night sky, during the night, share in a twenty four hour period, that is, twelve hours each. A regular solar calendar year has three hundred and sixty five days. A solar leap year has three hundred and sixty six days, a day added to the month of February every four years to make it have twenty nine days. This adjusts for the error because it takes about 365.25 days for the earth to rotate around the sun one revolution. It should also be mentioned that the Holy Spirit of God moved upon the face of the waters of earth, before God created the light and the sun (Gen. 1:2). So we must keep in mind Whom really rules over all of creation. Alleluia and praise the LORD. Amen and Amen.

It has been suggested that the original calendar had three hundred and sixty days in it, namely according to the number of months Noah and his family were in the Ark during the flood, one hundred and fifty of those days, seemingly being five, thirty day, months (Gen. 7:24).[3] It has been suggested that because of the change in the earth's form during and after the flood, that it may have slowed down the earth's rotation around the sun by about five and a quarter days each year. God only knows for certain. That all being said, the three hundred and sixty day year would be agreeable with a few prophecies in the New and Old Testament, namely regarding the "Great Tribulation", spoken of by Jesus, and John, through John's, Christ inspired vision, in the book of Revelation, and other prophets (Matt. 24:21, Rev. 2:22, 7:14, 11:3, 12:6). That being said, we must remember that Jesus Christ of Nazareth has fulfilled all scripture, regardless of prophetic scriptures regarding things to come. Albeit, Jesus did also say, that it would be like the days of Noe, when the coming of the Son of man is (Matt. 24:37). Nevertheless, there are also other references regarding the three hundred and sixty day year being used by Native Central American tribes.[4] It has been associated with various other empires in Eurasia, including the Romans and Greeks, and there are references online using a three hundred and sixty day year for calculations of financial investments.[5][6] This all being said, I think this shows, as much as anything, the challenge of calculating when Jesus Christ of Nazareth is going to "return" so to speak to earth, namely regarding when the "Great Tribulation" may take place, and other prophetic events Jesus spoke of, and the Holy Bible speaks of in general. As Jesus, Himself, said, "But of that day and hour knoweth no *man,* no, not the angels of heaven, but my Father only." (Matt. 24:36). He also

[1] https://en.wikipedia.org/wiki/Julian_calendar, retrieved 15/04/2022
[2] https://en.wikipedia.org/wiki/Julian_calendar#Replacement_by_the_Gregorian_calendar, retrieved 15/04/2022
[3] https://en.wikipedia.org/wiki/Prophetic_Year#History, retrieved 15/04/2022
[4] https://books.google.ca/books?id=2-cjAQAAIAAJ&pg=PA816&lpg=PA816&dq=Native+Central+American+tribes+use+360+day+year&source=bl&ots=2tlCf2oa6w&sig=ACfU3U2QkEeWJNUiaYcXUuTq5RERFMD3qg&hl=en&sa=X&ved=2ahUKEwinj5i245b3AhVBK80KHUmuCh8Q6AF6BAg6EAM#v=onepage&q=Native%20Central%20American%20tribes%20use%20360%20day%20year&f=false, retrieved 15/04/2022
[5] https://en.wikipedia.org/wiki/360-day_calendar, retrieved 15/04/2022
[6] https://www.investopedia.com/terms/d/daycount.asp, retrieved 15/04/2022

said of Himself to the apostle, John, in the book of Revelation, "Behold, I come as a thief. ..." (Rev. 16:15). Although I have speculated on the seasons of things regarding the "Great Tribulation", I would find it difficult to calculate exactly when. In this book, I will go into greater details about how Jesus fulfilled the scriptures regarding these things, and how God's calendar and Holy days are a shadow of things to come (Col. 2:17). To God be the glory in the truth of all of these things, in the name of His only begotten Son, Jesus Christ of Nazareth. Alleluia and praise the LORD. Amen and Amen.

Lesser

Genesis 1:16 says, "And God made two great lights; ...the lesser light to rule the night...". Of course, part of Jesus' final trial was during the night, before the morning of His crucifixion day (Matt. 26:31-34, 56-75). Nevertheless, Biblical Holy days and months are kept by the lunar calendar. And each month starts with a "new" moon, the first crescent moon seen after the moon is hidden from the sun, by the earth at the end of the month. The moon, just like the Hebrew language is read from right to left. That is, the first crescent of the new moon starts on the right side of the moon in the sky and works from right to left until the moon is full midway through the month, about the 14th or 15th day of the month in the lunar calendar system. The Hebrew calendar has thirty day months and twenty-nine day months. The Hebrew lunar calendar is adjusted seven times every nineteen years, in the solar calendar. An extra month, Adar I, is added every two to three years, depending on the adjustment needed.[7] Also, the 8th and 9th month of the Hebrew calendar, Bul/Heshvan and Chisleu/Kislev, can have 29 or 30 and 30 or 29 days, respectively. This range is used to adjust the calendar so that the Hebrew Holy days are celebrated on specific days of the week. The feast of Trumpets is used as a reference point, which is celebrated on the first day of the seventh month of the Hebrew calendar (Lev. 23:23-25). According to the Bible, the first day of the Hebrew year starts on the first day of the first month, Nisan, which is generally in the early spring in the northern hemisphere of the earth (Est. 3:7). All of this leads the possible range of the yearly calendar to include 353, 354 or 355 days in a normal lunar year, and 383, 384, or 385 days in a lunar leap year, with the extra month, Adar I, added as mentioned above. The lunar year is said to be; a deficient year, if it has 353 or 383 days; a regular year, if it has 354 or 384 days; and a complete year, if it has 355 or 385 days. See appendix A for more details about the lunar calendar, including an online reference regarding the greater details of how it functions. Alleluia and praise the LORD. Amen and Amen.

Today

Today much of the world uses the Gregorian calendar as a standard. But we have many different measures throughout the calendar year that mark the starts of the fiscal year, school year, calendar year, religious year, etc.. Not to mention, different cultures and nations, whom celebrate different "beginnings" of the year, as of the date of writing this book in 2019 A.D.. As far as I am concerned, the Bible is the ultimate reference for all truth including the beginning of the year, and according to the Bible, the beginning of the year corresponds to Nisan 1, which is usually in and around March or early April, depending on the year, according to the Gregorian calendar. As I had mentioned, the solar year and lunar year are recorded differently, see appendix B for more details on the differences

---

[7] http://www.jewfaq.org/calendar.htm, retrieved 15/04/2022

between the solar and lunar calendar year celebrations, and their respective history. Also, within Judaic "tradition", it seems that sometimes there is reference to two different times of the beginning of the year, the first being the Biblical beginning of the year, 1 Nisan, around March or April (Est. 3:7). For the fall reference to the beginning of the year, it is said that the creation of Adam and Eve, mark 1 Tishri/Ethanim, as the beginning of the year, which is in and around September or October time, but I personally have not found any Biblical evidence for this claim, although I suppose it is possible.[8] That being said, it has been suggested, and I would tend to agree, that Jesus was born on 1 Tishri/ Ethanim, the feast of Trumpets (Lev. 23:23-25, Luke 2:7-20).[9] I will go into greater detail about this in chapter five. The other interesting note is that there is a place in the Bible that marks the year of jubile, which is a year of release from bondage, redemption of property, and the like (Lev. 25:8-55). To announce the jubile year, the trumpet is blown on 10 Tishri/Ethanim, which is the Day of Atonement, in the scriptural Holy days (Lev. 23:26-32, Lev. 25:9, 10). Personally, I think the reason for this is to remind the Israelites, at least six months in advance, of the beginning of the coming jubile year. For practical purposes, it would be a reminder to the "rulers", that their servants may not be with them during the upcoming plowing, sowing and harvesting seasons, so they are given the opportunity to plan for the potential "labour shortages" (Lev. 25). This jubile or year of release happens every fifty years, and it has been suggested that one has taken place in 2016/17 A.D., to give a person an idea of where we may be at in that cycle.[10] The greater truth in this particular topic, is that Jesus Christ of Nazareth died for the forgiveness of our sins on the cross at Passover in 31 A.D., shedding His Holy and righteous blood. He was buried and He arose the third day and He has redeemed us from our sins and debts. As the Bible says, "…ye are bought with a price…" (1 Cor. 6:20). See appendix C for more details on the subject of the jubile. Alleluia and praise the LORD. Amen and Amen.

Conclusion

I am not going to tell a person how to live life, but I know that if God created something for a sign, then we should probably observe it. In particular, according to Ezekiel, it would seem that the feast of the "new" moon will be kept in the "Messianic Age" (Ezek. 45:17, 46:1, 3, 6). An aside; I purposely did not go into great detail of the calendars in this chapter, because I did not desire to confuse people. I am not an expert on the subject, and to be quite frank, the subject probably does not need to be any more complicated than any other subject of knowledge. Alleluia and praise the LORD. That being said, I did use the user edited, online encyclopedia, Wikipedia, and timeanddate.com for some references to both the solar and lunar calendar, in regards to historical development and the technical workings of both, as well as the online reference in appendix A and other online references. You can, at your own leisure, search out these subtopics; as the Bible admonishes us to "Prove all things; hold fast that which is good." (1 Thess. 5:21). And Jesus says, "…seek, and ye shall find…" (Matt. 7:7). Alleluia and praise the LORD. Amen and Amen.

---

[8] https://www.chabad.org/library/article_cdo/aid/4762/jewish/What-Is-Rosh-Hashanah.htm, retrieved 15/04/2022

[9] https://www.facebook.com/joeamaralpublic/posts/today-is-tishri-1-on-the-hebrew-calendar-its-known-as-rosh-hashanah-and-the-jewi/1712097898836485/, retrieved 15/04/2022

[10] https://www.linkedin.com/pulse/jubilee-year-2017-chadwick-harvey, retrieved 15/04/2022

Last, the lunar calendar is adjusted seven times in a nineteen year cycle. This could be reflective of the seven churches in the book of Revelation (Rev. 1-3). Five of those adjustments would be every three years and two of them would be every two years, equaling nineteen years, see appendix A for details. This may be reflective of the nature of the seven churches mentioned in the book of Revelation, where five of them seem to have needed more repentance (Rev. 2:1-7, 12-29; 3:1-6, 14-19). And two of them seem to not have fallen as far out of God's grace (Rev. 2:8-11, 3:7-13). This could be reflected in the Hebrew calendar, God knows. That being said, "…God is no respecter of persons…" (Acts. 10:34). And the most important thing to remember is that Jesus Christ of Nazareth came to earth, conceived by the Holy Spirit in and born of the virgin, Mary, espoused to Joseph (Matt. 1:18-25). He was born and raised a child of Israel, of the tribe of Judah, with brothers and sisters (Matt. 13:55, 56; Luke 2:41-52, Rev. 5:5). He began His earthly ministry at about the age of thirty in 27 A.D.; teaching, healing, forgiving and doing miracles for three and a half years (Luke 3:23). And at Passover in 31 A.D., He was crucified and died on the cross for the forgiveness of our sins, spilling His Holy and righteous blood. He was buried, and the third day He arose to give us the hope and promise of eternal life in His Holy name. Alleluia and praise the LORD. Amen and Amen. The next chapter will speak of the weekly Sabbath day of God, and go into greater detail of Jesus' crucifixion week, read on to learn more. Alleluia and praise the LORD. Amen and Amen.

Discussion: Time

"O LORD, I know that the way of man *is* not in himself: *it is*
not in man that walketh to direct his steps."
- Jeremiah 10:23

When I was considering my options and under review, during my last six month in the military, amongst other things, I had picked up the Bible that had been given to me by a relative in University. I had read up to 1 Chronicles in University, but the list of names became too tedious and boring for me to continue reading, so I stopped reading it. I know now, that the seemingly tedious and boring stuff in the Holy Bible is as important, as the more "interesting" passages. It is just that we all have a time for understanding and requiring certain knowledge about things in this world, so I suppose it was not my time to continue reading the Bible, at that time. At any rate, I started reading the Bible again in late 2009, early 2010 A.D., and I must have come to the passage above, or else I just randomly flipped to it. The situation was such, that I drove my vehicle, at the time, to a local conservation area on the outskirts of the town I was living in, and I walked some distance through the trails and into the woods for some peace and quiet. I took this Bible I was reading, from University, with me; it was the New International Version, for the reader's information. I sat down under a tree and flipped to Jeremiah 10:23, although I may have been reading other verses at the time, I do not remember. Nevertheless, my attention was drawn to Jeremiah 10:23, and I kept reading it over and over again, the sun was just above the tree line in the distance, in the west, and it was around winter time, as there were a few centimeters of snow on the ground. At the time, the meaning of the verse did not mean that much to me, but I must have repeated it so many times that it has been etched into my memory. It has served me well in remembering that God is indeed sovereign over all things, and it is a reminder that both the New Testament and the Old Testament agree on this. Alleluia and praise the LORD. Amen and Amen.

Discussion Questions

1. Is Jesus the Messiah, the Saviour of the world, and the prophesied eternal King over Israel?

    _____

    _____

    _____

2. Hate and the sword and division are all mentioned by Jesus in His ministry, mostly in reference to family, although He did mention that His followers would be hated by all (Matt. 10:22). The question is then, what did He mean in these various circumstances, and how does that "hate" affect our lives here on earth?

    _____

    _____

    _____

CHAPTER 2

The Sabbath

"And on the seventh day God ended his work which he had made; and he
rested on the seventh day from all his work which he had made."
- Genesis 2:2

Introduction

Much understanding of the New and Old Testament scriptures is determined by understanding and following the command to keep the Sabbath day holy (Gen. 2:3). Without knowing and keeping the proper day, as a holy and rest day, each week; the prophetic nature of Scripture starts to crumble, because of disobedience to this one simple yet perpetual command (Ex. 31:16). That being said, the New Testament says, "Rejoice in the Lord alway...", "Pray without ceasing", etc. (Phil. 4:4, 1 Thess. 5:17). In the beginning God created the heavens and the earth and on the seventh day He rested, not only that but He sanctified the seventh day, that means, He made it Holy (Gen. 1, 2:1-3). God used signs, similitudes and practical examples to teach the ancient Israelites how to follow His laws and commands; like collecting manna in the wilderness six days, with a double portion collected on the sixth day to supply for the seventh day as well, in order to rest from work on the seventh day (Ex. 16, Ex. 20:1-17). However, in the wilderness and after the Israelites entered into the "promised land", and had judges and then kings over them, the tribes began to "fall away" from God's commands (Ex. 16:19, 20, 27-29; 32:1-8; Jud. 18, 1 Kings 12). Jeroboam, the king of the northern tribes of Israel, setup his own altars in northern Israel and instituted a feast day, outside of God's commands in Leviticus 23 (1 Kings 12:26-33). And partially as a consequence, the northern tribes of Israel eventually went into captivity by the Assyrians in about 700 B.C., and lost their Hebrew identities (2 Kings 15:29, 17:4-23, 18:9-12). I say, partially, because the descendants of all of the tribes of Israel were prophesied to be at the "...ends of the earth...", in the "...last days...", in order to fulfil God's greater plans for the descendants of Israel, and the whole world in general (Gen. 49, Deut. 33:17). The "Jews", the tribe of Judah, kept the commands, but also went into captivity, to the Babylonians in about 550 B.C., because of rebellion against God, and are likely mostly the modern day "Jews" of today, as of the date of writing this book in 2019 A.D. (2 Kings 24, 25). Hosea 11:12 says, "...Judah yet ruleth with God, and is faithful with the saints.". Jesus came to reach the lost tribes of Israel, whom are scattered abroad; generally, the European and English nations whom founded western societies today (Matt. 10:6, Jam. 1:1). Jesus came not only for the lost sheep of Israel, but for the entire world (John 10:16). And He declares that He is Lord of the Sabbath (Mark 2:28). So, with that all being said; let's read on and learn more about this so called day of rest, the "Sabbath". Alleluia and praise the LORD. Amen and Amen.

Which day?

The meaning of the word, sabbath, is rest; Strong's number 7676 and the root, Strong's number 7673 (Gen. 2:2, Ex. 16:23). And the purpose of it, Mark 2:27 and 28 say, "…The sabbath was made for man, and not man for the sabbath: Therefore the Son of man is Lord also of the sabbath.". The purpose is for our rest and refreshment after working the previous six days (Ex. 31:17). The seventh day, Sabbath, command was given in the beginning (Gen. 2:2, 3). The Sabbath command was again given after the Passover and days of unleavened bread command given in Egypt, during the exodus, but before the Ten Commandments in the wilderness (Ex. 16, Ex. 31:12-17). The Sabbath command was given again in the Ten Commandments at Mount Horeb in the wilderness, and is listed fourth in the commandments, before six other commands (Ex. 20:8-11). The point in all of this is, that the seventh day, Sabbath, command has not changed and will never change, as God does not change (Mal. 3:6). Exodus 31:12 and 13 say, "And the LORD spake unto Moses, saying, Speak thou also unto the children of Israel, saying, Verily my Sabbaths ye shall keep: for it *is* a sign between me and you throughout your generations; that *ye* may know that I *am* the LORD that doth sanctify you.". This is part of the key to knowing the true God, by keeping His commands. One of those commands is keeping the seventh day, Sabbath day, holy, by resting. This should not be seen as a burden, but a blessing. Alleluia and praise the LORD. Amen and Amen.

God desires us not to go after our own ways and desires on the Sabbath day, but to follow Him and rest (Isa. 58:13, 14). He has given us six other days for walking after our own ways; but the seventh day, He desires us to turn to Him as the Creator and worship Him, sanctify Him. The manna in the wilderness is a perfect example of this, so was Jesus' miracles with the fishes and the loaves (Ex. 16, Matt. 14:15-21, 15:32-38). Why do we work? To gain money, food, and provisions in general; so we can provide for ourselves and others as required. If God proves in the wilderness that He is the ultimate provider, and proved this again with Jesus Christ of Nazareth, should we not listen? Why ought we to keep disobeying God and carrying out our own fleshly desires on the day the Lord created for us to rest and keep holy? To me there is no reason for it. The Old Testament has an example of a leader of Israel having to close the gates and turn foreign traders away from the gates of Jerusalem in order to maintain the seventh day, Sabbath, within the city (Neh. 13:15-22). Albeit, in the "…new Jerusalem…", the gates will always be open, but this is a spiritual vision of God saying that we can always come to Him (Rev. 21:25). That being said, there is an angel at each gate in the vision (Rev.21:12). And Jesus said of Himself, "…I am the door…" (John 10:7). We are saved by entering in to the kingdom of God, through Jesus Christ of Nazareth (John 10:9). And this access has been given to us through Jesus Christ of Nazareth dying on the cross for the forgiveness of our sins at Passover in 31 A.D., spilling His Holy and righteous blood. He was buried and the third day He arose to give us the hope and promise of eternal life in His Holy name. Alleluia and praise the LORD. Amen and Amen.

The key to keeping the Sabbath, Holy, is related to obedience; because it requires us to turn away from our own desires and lusts in order to serve God. Which ought to be done daily, but God has given us one day a week for rest, outside of whatever work we take on during the work week. This has to do with economy, money, consumption and every other evil that we can partake in, in this world. Jesus healed on the Sabbath, that was not sin, because healing is not sin (Matt. 12:10-12). However, if we are working selfishly on the Sabbath, as with any day, it is sin (1 Cor. 10:31, Col. 3:17, 23). Not only this, but God created this day for rest (Gen. 2:2, 3). If God desired to rest, and we were created in His image, we ought to follow His example and rest, as well (Gen. 1:26, 27; 2:2, 3). Jews celebrate the Sabbath on Saturday and so do some Christian organizations, as of the date of writing this book in 2019 A.D.. The calendar working week starts on Monday, and ends on Friday, generally, in the West. But things have changed throughout the centuries. In the Bible, it warns of those who would attempt to change times, and laws (Dan. 7:25). The fact of the matter is, the Biblical times and laws have not changed. Jesus did not come to destroy the law but to fulfill it (Matt. 5:17). He is the end of the law (Rom. 10:4). He is the perfection of the law. Did Jesus' disciples pick, glean grain for food on the Sabbath? Yes. Did Jesus heal on the Sabbath? Yes. But this was not to break the Sabbath command. If Jesus was, and is, perfect and He died on the cross for the forgiveness of our sins, shedding His Holy and righteous blood. He was buried and He arose the third day for our hope and promise of eternal life in His Holy name. Then that means; He did not break the Sabbath command either, neither did He break any other laws of the Old Testament. This may be hard to believe for some, but it is the reality. Jesus did not come to condemn the world, but to save it (John 3:17). And He certainly did not come to change the day of the week for the Sabbath. It has, and always will, be the 7th day of the week and if calendars and time keepers are generally correct, then it must be Saturday, according to the Gregorian calendar system. Alleluia and praise the LORD. Amen and Amen.

To understand this in greater detail, one must understand that the Hebrews use the moon as well as the sun to calculate the months and days, as spoken of in chapter one. The moon is a greater indicator of the beginning of the month, the seasons indicate the time of the year and the Sabbath is related to all of this. I am not an expert in time keeping, but I know that if God has set some people to keep watch over the times and seasons, year after year, for thousands of years, certainly He can do this and has. Of course, the other side of the coin is that faith is required to follow Jesus Christ of Nazareth and the truth of God, in general. I could explain away an idea until the cows come home, but the reality is in Jesus Christ of Nazareth. As the Bible says, "Rejoice in the Lord alway..." (Phil. 4:4). But for those who argue against the truth for their own agenda, this is where things get dangerous. The truth is the truth and for those God is revealing the truth to, it can be done with as you please, but God will hold you accountable for it. Just like we are all given responsibilities in this world, we must also, take responsibility for the truth that God reveals to each and every one of us. This is why I have written this book. Alleluia and praise the LORD. Amen and Amen.

Jesus' Crucifixion

It has been suggested that Jesus was crucified on a Wednesday; in these next two paragraphs I will go through the evidence for this.[11] It will be shown by various verses throughout the four gospels around the time of Jesus' crucifixion, burial and resurrection that His fleshly body was indeed lifeless for three days and nights in a tomb, as told by Him using the sign of Jonah (Matt. 12:40). First let us start at the Passover supper, the night of His betrayal. The night of His betrayal, He spent time at Passover supper with His disciples, at which time He figuratively gave up His life, by answering Judas what

---

[11] https://rcg.org/articles/ccwnof.html, retrieved 18/04/2022

he must do (Matt. 26:25). Although His physical body was still alive, He would have almost certainly felt death lingering around Him. This was the beginning of His ultimate understanding and feeling of taking all of our sins upon Himself, as the eternal Passover lamb (Matt. 26:38). His conversations with God, the Father, make this very evident (Mark 14:36). The next morning He was given into the hands of His accusers and prepared for physical death on the cross for the forgiveness of our sins (Mark 14:41). This day was still the day of Passover, as a Hebrew day always starts the night before (Gen. 1:5). So Jesus Christ of Nazareth was physically crucified on the Passover day and physically died on the cross around the 9th hour, 3 pm (Mark 15:34, John 18:39). Now, Jesus was prepared for burial, then laid in a new tomb owned by a faithful believer, Joseph (Luke 23:53, John 19:41, 42). The day after, was a Special Jewish Sabbath day, a high day, which is not to be confused with the weekly Sabbath that the Jews observe on Saturday. This High day in particular was the first day of Unleavened bread (John 19:31). The days of unleavened bread will be spoken of in greater detail in the next chapter. Alleluia and praise the LORD. Amen and Amen.

After this, was another preparation day in which Mary, Mary Magdalene and Salome bought some spices to prepare to anoint Jesus' body in the tomb (Mark 16:1). They were again, buying these spices the day before a Sabbath, but not a High day, likely the weekly Sabbath, Saturday (Luke 23:56). Now, Mary Magdalene and Mary with others went to the tomb early on the first day of the week and Jesus was already risen (Luke 24:1). Praise God. If we work our way backward from that morning or better later the night before and remember that His death on the cross took place at 3pm on a certain day of the week (Mark 15:34). A good educated guess of His crucifixion day would be Wednesday. As the sign of Jonah goes, He would have had three days; Thursday, Friday and Saturday, and three nights; Thursday night, Friday night and Saturday night, having been resurrected before the women made it to the tomb early Sunday morning (Luke 24:1-3). However, there is a disconnect, because Wednesday night is unaccounted for, but maybe this is part of the mystery. No matter, there is going to be some imperfect explanation through my words. The truth requires faith, and as the Bible says of God, "For *as* the heavens are higher than the earth, so are my ways higher than your ways..." (Isa. 55:9). So, this is an interpretation of the events, however, remember as the Bible says, "Prove all things; hold fast that which is good." (1 Thess. 5:21). The challenge of suggesting that Friday was the crucifixion day is that Jesus would not have had three full days in the tomb. He would have had closer to one and maybe a couple hours on Friday, and if any, maybe a few minutes or an hour before the women came to the tomb Sunday morning. So depending on how Scripture is interpreted and what Jesus meant by "three days", the argument below may also be considered. However, if He meant three twelve hour days, which I would argue He did, then the Wednesday crucifixion is much more likely. See appendix D – Jesus' crucifixion and resurrection week timeline for visual detail of the timeline and events. Alleluia and praise the LORD. Amen and Amen.

With that all being said, there is some evidence that would suggest Jesus was "resurrected" Sunday. Namely, in Mark 16:9, it says, "Now when *Jesus* was risen early the first *day* of the week, he appeared first to Mary Magdalene...". However if a comma was placed after "...risen...", it would read differently. Also, a more difficult Scripture to argue against is Luke 24:21, it says, "But we trusted that it had been he which should have redeemed Israel: and beside all this, to day is the third day since these things were done." (Luke 24:1). Although the gospel writer, Luke, said his understanding was perfect regarding the events (Luke 1:1-4). I have found Luke's record of the accuracy of the timing of events to be the least agreeable with the other three gospel records of Matthew, Mark and John.

As well, Luke, does not seem to be one of the original twelve apostles, following Jesus, during His earthly ministry, unless his name was changed, so it is possible that even Luke received information from other people regarding the events he recorded. The point of all of this, is to suggest that it is possible Jesus was crucified on a Wednesday and He spent three nights and three days in the grave, being resurrected sometime Saturday, when no one was aware (Luke 24:1-3). But it is possible that the third day was Sunday, and He was somehow crucified a day after Wednesday. Popular tradition has it that He was crucified on Friday, as of the date of writing this book in 2019 A.D.; but a good disciple of Jesus needs to, as the Bible says, "Prove all things; hold fast that which is good." (1 Thess. 5:21). There must be a truth to all of this, and certainly the majority of the population whom celebrate "Easter", would argue against a Wednesday crucifixion, as of the date of writing this book in 2019 A.D.. However, regardless of when He was crucified, He did indeed say that He was going to be in the grave for three days and three nights, using the sign of Jonah being in the belly of the whale for three days and three nights (Matt. 12:40). So we must ask ourselves, what is the truth? Simply the truth is that the crucifixion took place and that Jesus Christ of Nazareth died on the cross for the forgiveness of our sins at Passover in 31 A.D., spilling His Holy and righteous blood. He was buried and He arose the third day to give us the promise of eternal life in His Holy name. There may be more details to the historical account of the truth of His crucifixion, burial and resurrection, but we must not miss the simple message of salvation in the life, death on the cross for the forgiveness of our sins, burial and resurrection of Jesus Christ of Nazareth. Alleluia and praise the LORD. Amen and Amen.

Saturday vs. Sunday

The idea of Sunday being a sabbath, as I understand, comes from a few places in the New Testament teachings. The first being that people claim, that Jesus was resurrected on the 1st day of the week, although Mary came to the tomb on the first day of the week (Matt. 28:1, Mark 16:2, 9; Luke 24:1, John 20:1). There is little place in the New Testament that would indicate Jesus was actually resurrected on the first day of the week; save Mark 16:9, "Now when *Jesus* was risen early the first *day* of the week, he appeared first to Mary Magdalene…". However if a comma or period was placed after "… risen…", it would read differently. In fact, as I had mentioned in the previous section, Jesus was very likely resurrected Saturday, in the afternoon at some point, or sometime before light on "Sunday". Jesus arising early the first day of the week is the main argument for keeping Sunday as the "Sabbath", by many today, claiming it to be the "Lord's Day". But the actual "Lord's Day" or the "day of the Lord" mentioned in the Bible, is about a terrible time of vengeance and punishment on this world. At the culmination of what the Bible calls the "Great Tribulation", also related to the final judgement of earth's inhabitants (Acts 2:20, 1 Cor. 5:5, 2 Cor. 1:14, 1 Tim. 5:2, 2 Pet. 3:10, Rev. 1:10). This time is mentioned in various places throughout the Bible, as the "…day of the LORD…", the "…year of recompences…", the "…day of wrath…", etc. (Isa. 2:12, 13:6, 9; 34:8, Jer. 46:10, Ezek. 13:5, 30:3; Joel 1:15, 2:1, 11, 31; 3:14; Amos 5:18, 20; Obad. 1:15, Zeph. 1:7, 8, 14, 15, 18; 2:2, 3; Zech. 14:1, Mal. 4:5). Albeit, Jesus did fulfill the vengeance of God toward sinful man, on the cross, as we receive Him. The other argument is that the disciples came together on the first day of the week, after the resurrection to fellowship and to offer collections (Luke 24, John 20:19, Acts 20:7, 1 Cor. 16:2). The apostle, Paul, said, "Upon the first *day* of the week let every one of you lay by him in store, as *God* hath prospered him, that there be no gatherings when I come." (1 Cor. 16:2). Nevertheless, Hebrews 4 goes into detail about the topic, in Hebrews 4:8, it says, "For if Jesus had given them rest, then would he not afterward have spoken of another day.". This also may be referencing the "Messianic Age", or 1000 years of Christ's rule with His saints (Rev. 20:4, 6). The point is, we can rest in Jesus, as He has removed our burdens, but He did not come to change the day of weekly rest (Matt. 11:28). Alleluia and praise the LORD. Amen and Amen.

The other evidence that scholars use to claim that Sunday is "the Lord's day", is that they took up some sort of collection on the first day of the week, as mentioned. Also, the apostle, Paul, preached late into the night Sunday until midnight; at one point (Acts 20:7). For the number of times it is mentioned that the apostles and Jesus preached in the synagogues on the Sabbath, Saturday, compared to the number of times it is mentioned that the New Testament Church gathered on Sunday, there is little comparison. The other suggestion is that the purpose for moving Christian worship to Sunday was to differentiate the Christian Church from Judaism, this may have been the "reasoning" by some, including the Roman Emperor, Constantine.[12] But the reality is, it was exactly this type of people that Jesus and the apostles warned about. Whether the counsel of Nicea did it ignorantly or willfully, is hard to speculate, as the heart of the king is in the hand of God (Prov. 21:1). However, when it comes to following man or God, I would and Jesus Christ of Nazareth admonishes us to, follow God, the true Father, and Himself, Jesus Christ of Nazareth, through His Holy Spirit; given to all whom receive Him freely. So if you are seriously considering and attempting to understand what to do about which day you set aside for rest; take time, meditate and pray about it. Ultimately, Jesus Christ of Nazareth desires a personal relationship with each and every one of us, regardless of whether we attend a fellowship, take a break on a specific day, etc.. But certainly there are benefits to taking rest, so seriously consider when and how often you should have it. Alleluia and praise the LORD. Amen and Amen.

Conclusion

Philippians 4:4 says, "Rejoice in the Lord alway…". God is not calling us to be "righteous" and good, one day of the week. The point of the Sabbath is for rest. God desires us always to worship Him, pray, and learn from Him. Just like everything else on earth, man has managed to manipulate and pervert the very purpose of the Sabbath, for our own selfish gain and reasons. The Sabbath, from the beginning, was simply put, created for rest. The day is sanctified by us resting, not toiling in evils, selfish gain, etc.. Jesus Christ of Nazareth is Lord of the Sabbath, and the Sabbath was made for man, not man for the Sabbath (Mark 2:27, 28). God rested on the seventh day of His creation (Gen. 2:2, 3). The Israelites collected manna six days and rested on the seventh day in the wilderness (Ex. 16). The Sabbath is a perpetual covenant and it points to the "Messianic Age", the millennial reign of Christ and His saints, and ultimately points to the completion of God's plan for mankind here on this earth, which is peace and rest for all of mankind (Ex. 31:16, Heb. 4). Alleluia and praise the LORD. Amen and Amen.

Exodus 31:12-17 says, "And the LORD spake unto Moses, saying, Speak thou also unto the children of Israel, saying, Verily my Sabbaths ye shall keep: for it *is* a sign between me and you throughout your generations; that *ye* may know that I *am* the LORD that doth sanctify you. Ye shall keep the sabbath therefore; for it *is* holy unto you: every one that defileth it shall surely be put to death: for whosoever doeth *any* work therein, that soul shall be cut off from among his people. Six days may work be done;

---

[12] https://www.cgi.org/who-changed-the-sabbath-to-sunday, retrieved 18/04/2022

but in the seventh *is* the sabbath of rest, holy to the LORD: whosoever doeth *any* work in the sabbath day, he shall surely be put to death. Wherefore the children of Israel shall keep the sabbath, to observe the sabbath throughout their generations, *for* a perpetual covenant. It *is* a sign between me and the children of Israel for ever: for *in* six days the LORD made heaven and earth, and on the seventh day he rested, and was refreshed.". Alleluia and praise the LORD. Amen and Amen.

The laws of God are not for the fleshly descendants of the Israelites only; the law of God is for all of mankind, even according to the law of God, as "...God is no respecter of persons..." (Num. 15:29, Acts 10:34). The law of God is Good and Holy (Rom. 3, 7). That being said, we are not justified by our works in the law, but we are justified by Jesus Christ of Nazareth's works in the law, as He came to fulfil the law and the prophets (Matt. 5:17, Gal. 3:11, Eph. 2:8, 9). It is by Jesus Christ of Nazareth, that we are saved, forgiven, redeemed and healed. It is by Jesus Christ of Nazareth, and His death on the cross at Passover in 31 A.D., for the forgiveness of our sins, that we are justified and forgiven. It is by Jesus Christ of Nazareth spilling His Holy and righteous blood on the cross that we are cleansed from our sins. And it is by Jesus Christ of Nazareth's, burial, and His resurrection three days later that we have hope and a promise of eternal life in His Holy name. Alleluia and praise the LORD. Amen and Amen. The next four chapters will speak about the annual Holy days of God, spoken of in Leviticus 23 and instituted as the Israelites were being brought out of captivity from the Egyptians and into their wilderness journey of forty years, while preparing to enter their "promised land" (Ex. 12, Lev. 23). The following chapters will also speak about the annual Holy days and their relevance in the Old Testament, in Jesus' day, today, and for things to come, read on to learn more. Alleluia and praise the LORD. Amen and Amen.

Discussion: Sabbath

"For the LORD thy God walketh in the midst of thy camp, to deliver thee,
and to give up thine enemies before thee; therefore shall thy camp be holy:
that he see no unclean thing in thee, and turn away from thee."
- Deuteronomy 23:14

It should be mentioned that the apostle, Paul, mentions, "For all have sinned and come short of the glory of God.", as is similarly mentioned in two Old Testament Psalms (Ps. 14:1, 3; 53:1, 3; Rom. 3:23). That being said, Jesus also admonishes us to be perfect, even as our Father in Heaven is perfect (Matt. 5:48). He also says, that if our righteousness does not exceed that of the scribes and Pharisees, we will not enter into the kingdom of God (Matt. 5:20). This is why the Bible can be interpreted, and why various scholars have speculated about the validity of, any one translation of the Holy Bible of God. That being said, if we truly believe there is a God, and that He is the Creator, then we need not worry or be anxious about interpretations, translations, etc.. Jesus said that He, Himself, is the way, the truth and the life (John 14:6). If He is the truth, and He has given us His Holy Spirit, which is truthful, then God, the Father, through His Holy Spirit, in the name of His only begotten Son, Jesus Christ of Nazareth, will lead us into all truth, as Jesus said (John 16:13). The truth is that in order for Deuteronomy 23:14 above to be fulfilled, we need Jesus Christ of Nazareth. He is the only man, conceived by the Holy Spirit of God, in and born to the virgin, Mary, espoused to Joseph, of the tribe of Judah, of the house of David, born a sinless man (Matt. 1:18-25, Rev. 5:5). He had brothers and sisters, and was raised as a child of Israel (Matt. 13:55, 56; Luke 2:41-52). He began His ministry at the age of about thirty years old and for three and a half years, did miracles, preached, ministered, healed and forgave sins, as a sinless man (Luke 3:23). And at Passover in 31 A.D., He died on the cross for the forgiveness of our sins, shedding His Holy and righteous blood. He was buried and the third day He arose to give us the hope and promise of eternal life in His Holy name. Alleluia and praise the LORD. Amen and Amen.

Discussion Questions

1. The knowledge of all of these different signs and the Holy Days of God are great, and ought to be followed, if done in the Spirit of Jesus Christ of Nazareth. But what is the reality of all of this?

_____

_____

_____

2. What about idols? What can they teach us?

_____

_____

_____

CHAPTER 3

Passover and Feast of Unleavened Bread

"Great peace have they which love thy law: and nothing shall offend them."
- Psalm 119:165

Introduction

The Holy days of the Bible are said to be a shadow of things to come (Col. 2:16, 17). This is the simplest and easiest way to explain the purpose of them. They are a way of keeping track of time, but are also a sign of things to come; if they are understood in the greater plan, God has been working out, here on earth, and has revealed to man, through His prophets and saints. That is, God's plan of repentance, redemption and salvation of all of mankind here on earth from all of earth's history. Many of the prophets spoke of their redemption and salvation. All prophets were called to preach repentance for the remission of sins by God, but Jesus Christ of Nazareth actually went further, and gave His life as an atoning sacrifice for the forgiveness of our sins. Something no other prophet or man of God has ever done, as He was, and is, Holy and perfect. Conceived in late 5 B.C.; by the Holy Spirit in and born of the virgin Mary, espoused to Joseph, in the fall of 4 B.C. (Matt. 1:18-25). He was raised, a child of Israel, with brothers and sisters (Matt. 13:55, 56; Luke 2:41-52). He began His earthly ministry at about the age of thirty years old, and preached the kingdom of God; He healed, forgave and did other miracles for three and a half years (Luke 3:23). And at Passover in 31 A.D., He gave up His life on the cross for the forgiveness of our sins, spilling His Holy and righteous blood, He died on the cross. He was buried and three days later He was redeemed to God through His resurrection power, giving us the hope and promise of the forgiveness of our sins and newness of life in this life and the resurrection of our redeemed body, soul and spirit, in the world to come. With this simple explanation of the purpose of the Holy days explained in the life, death and resurrection of Jesus Christ of Nazareth, let us go into greater detail about each Holy day, their purposes and meanings in history, today and in the years to come. This chapter speaks of the Holy days of Passover and the feast of unleavened bread, read on to learn more. Alleluia and praise the LORD. Amen and Amen.

Passover

Leviticus 23:5 says, "In the fourteenth *day* of the first month at even *is* the LORD's passover.". The Passover account of Exodus 12:1-14 says, "And the LORD spake unto Moses and Aaron in the land of Egypt saying, This month *shall be* unto you the beginning of months: it shall be the first month of the year to you. Speak ye unto all the congregation of Israel, saying, In the tenth *day* of this month they shall take to them every man a lamb, according to the house of *their* fathers, a lamb for an house: And if the household be too little for the lamb, let him and his neighbor next unto his house take *it* according to the number of the souls; every man according to his eating shall make your count for the lamb. Your lamb shall be without blemish, a male of the first year: ye shall take *it* out from the sheep, or from the goats: And ye shall keep it up until the fourteenth day of the same month: and the whole assembly of the congregation of Israel shall kill it in the evening. And they shall take of the blood, and strike *it* on the two side posts and on the upper door post of the houses, wherein they shall eat it. And they shall eat the flesh in that night, roast with fire, and unleavened bread; *and* with bitter *herbs* they shall eat it. Eat not of it raw, nor sodden at all with water, but roast *with* fire; his head with his legs, and with the purtenance thereof. And ye shall let nothing of it remain until the morning; and that which remaineth of it until the morning ye shall burn with fire. And thus shall ye eat it; *with* your loins girded, your shoes on your feet, and your staff in your hand; and ye shall eat it in haste: it *is* the LORD's passover. For I will pass through the land of Egypt this night, and will smite all the firstborn in the land of Egypt, both man and beast; and against all the gods of Egypt I will execute judgment: I *am* the LORD. And the blood shall be to you for a token upon the houses where ye *are:* and when I see the blood, I will pass over you, and the plague shall not be upon you to destroy *you,* when I smite the land of Egypt. And this day shall be unto you for a memorial; and ye shall keep it a feast to the LORD throughout your generations; ye shall keep it a feast by an ordinance for ever.". Alleluia and praise the LORD. Amen and Amen.

Exodus 12:21-32 says, "Then Moses called for all the elders of Israel, and said unto them, Draw out and take you a lamb according to your families, and kill the passover. And ye shall take a bunch of hyssop, and dip *it* in the blood that *is* in the bason, and strike the lintel and the two side posts with the blood that *is* in the bason; and none of you shall go out at the door of his house until the morning. For the LORD will pass through to smite the Egyptians; and when he seeth the blood upon the lintel, and on the two side posts, the LORD will pass over the door, and will not suffer the destroyer to come in unto your houses to smite *you.* And ye shall observe this thing for an ordinance to thee and to thy sons for ever. And it shall come to pass, when ye be come to the land which the LORD will give you, according as he hath promised, that ye shall keep this service. And it shall come to pass, when your children shall say unto you, What mean ye by this service? That ye shall say, It *is* the sacrifice of the LORD's passover, who passed over the houses of the children of Israel in Egypt, when he smote the Egyptians, and delivered our houses. And the people bowed the head and worshipped. And the children of Israel went away, and did as the LORD had commanded Moses and Aaron, so did they. And it came to pass, that at midnight the LORD smote all the firstborn in the land of Egypt, from the firstborn of Pharaoh that sat on his throne unto the firstborn of the captive that *was* in the dungeon; and all the firstborn of cattle. And Pharaoh rose up in the night, he, and all his servants, and all the Egyptians; and there was a great cry in Egypt; for *there was* not a house where *there was* not one dead. And he called for Moses and Aaron by night, and said, Rise up, *and* get you forth from among my people, both ye and the children of Israel; and go, serve the LORD, as ye have said. Also take your flocks and your herds, as ye have said, and be gone; and bless me also.". The description of this historical event will continue in the next section as the days of unleavened bread, of course, the Holy Bible will give you the full account of this, as well. Alleluia and praise the LORD. Amen and Amen.

Jesus partook in Passover as a boy, at 12 years old, in about 10 A.D., with His parents in Jerusalem (Luke 2:41-52). Jesus submitted to the authority of His parents, as is commanded in the Old Testament laws, and Jesus confirmed in His teachings (Luke 2:51). Since Passover ought to point to Christ Jesus of Nazareth and His offering for us, let's discuss this day in 31 A.D., when Christ gave His life for us. The evening before, His disciples prepared a place to eat the Passover meal, in a house in Jerusalem; at this meal, He told His disciples about His betrayal and commanded for Judas to do it quickly, and Judas left to do so (Matt. 26:17-25, John 13:27-30). This is where the bread and the wine were established as a memorial in eating and drinking for what He has done for us, in giving us His flesh and blood shed on the cross for the forgiveness of our sins (Matt. 26:26-28). He and His disciples, after the meal, went to the garden of Gethsemane to pray (Matt. 26:36). At this time, Jesus spoke very intimately with God, the Father, and asked if the cup of sacrifice could be taken from Him, but Jesus ultimately said to God, the Father, "...thy will be done." (Matt. 26:42). Soon after this, Judas and the authorities came to take Him (Matt. 26:47, 48). I will say one thing about Judas, positively, he told the authorities to take Jesus away safely (Mark 14:44). Jesus was then tried and crucified at the 3rd hour, 9am, and He died on the cross at the 9th hour, 3pm, on 14 Nisan in 31 A.D. (Mark 15:25, 34). Soon after this, His body was taken down from the cross and given to Joseph of Arimathea, whom prepared Jesus' body with burial cloth and placed Him in a new tomb, likely in the garden tomb in Jerusalem, as known today (Mark 15:42-46). Alleluia and praise the LORD. Amen and Amen.

Exodus 12:40-51 speaks of how strangers are not to partake in the Passover, and if they dwell amongst Israel, they must be circumcised to take part (Ex. 12:43-45). Putting this into proper perspective in the light of Jesus Christ of Nazareth, we need to look at the spiritual side of these commands. God is looking for people whom are circumcised in the heart. This is mentioned, in both the Old and New Testament (1 Sam. 16:7, Col. 2:10-12). This is the circumcision of the Holy Spirit, through receiving the offering of Jesus Christ of Nazareth's forgiveness for our sins, by His shed blood on the cross at Passover in 31 A.D.. It may sound simple, but it is the truth. As the apostle, Paul, spoke, "There is neither Jew nor Greek, there is neither bond nor free, there is neither male nor female: for ye are all one in Christ Jesus." (Gal. 3:28). This is the common offering Jesus Christ of Nazareth made to all, fulfilling what the psalmist said of God, "...thy commandment *is* exceeding broad." (Ps. 119:96). Although life in Jesus Christ of Nazareth is simple and narrow, the life before knowing Jesus as your Saviour might have been "...exceeding broad." (Ps. 119:96, Matt. 7:14). As Jesus said, "Enter ye in at the strait gate: for wide *is* the gate, and broad is the way, that leadeth to destruction..." (Matt. 7:13). This is why Jesus died for all of mankind, so that the laws of God would be fulfilled (Matt. 5:17). Seek Jesus Christ of Nazareth and accept His offering of eternal life in His Holy name, through His sacrifice on the cross, and you will find your salvation, and you will find truth. I promise you this. He died on the cross at Passover in 31 A.D., spilling His Holy and righteous blood on the cross. He was buried and the third day He arose to give us the hope and promise of eternal life in His Holy name. Alleluia and praise the LORD. Amen and Amen.

Exodus 12:46 says, "In one house shall it be eaten; thou shalt not carry forth ought of the flesh abroad out of the house; neither shall ye break a bone thereof.". This was prophesied of Jesus, later by the psalmist, King David (Ps. 34:20). Not a bone was broken in Jesus' body on the cross (John 19:36). John the Baptist, in the gospel according to John, spoke of Jesus, as the Lamb of God (John 1:29, 36). The apostle, John, wrote in the book of Revelation, speaking in greater detail of Jesus, as the Passover lamb (Rev. 5:6, 8, 12, 13; 6:1, 16; 7:9, 10, 14, 17; 12:11, 13:8, 14:1, 4, 10; 15:3, 17:14, 19:7, 9; 21:9, 14, 22, 23, 27; 22:1, 3). Revelation 5:12 says, "...Worthy is the Lamb that was slain to receive power, and riches, and wisdom, and strength, and honour, and glory, and blessing.". Exodus 12:23 says, "For the LORD will pass through to smite the Egyptians; and when he seeth the blood upon the lintel, and on the two side posts, the LORD will pass over the door, and will not suffer the destroyer to come in unto your houses to smite *you*.". Accepting the blood of Jesus Christ of Nazareth into our life and washing ourselves clean with His offering does the same thing, but in a greater way than what God did for Israel in the Exodus example. The sacrifice of the lamb and the application of its blood on the door posts for protection was a sign and a foreshadowing of Christ dying on the cross for the forgiveness of our sin (Rev. 7:14). It is by the blood of Jesus Christ of Nazareth, that we have been passed over; we have passed from sin and death to resurrection and a life, that is, life everlasting in Jesus Christ of Nazareth's Holy name (Rev. 12:11). Alleluia and praise the LORD. Amen and Amen. Applying this to things to come regarding the "Messianic Age", would be the same for most people, as it is today. But in the "bigger picture", if there is to be a temple built in Jerusalem, on Mount Moriah, where the first and second temples were built. Then it is very possible, that at some point in time in the future, we will indeed be able to experience something similar to what the Old Testament Israelites did during Passover; slaying the Passover lamb and eating it in remembrance of things that have been. This is mentioned in Ezekiel 45:21. No matter, we must always put Jesus Christ of Nazareth first and foremost in mind, and what He has done for us on the cross, that is, offering up His body for the forgiveness of our sins on the cross at Passover in 31 A.D., spilling His Holy and righteous blood, He died on the cross. He was buried and the third day He arose to give us the hope and promise of eternal life in His Holy name. Alleluia and praise the LORD. Amen and Amen.

Feast of Unleavened Bread

Leviticus 23:6-8 says, "And on the fifteenth day of the same month *is* the feast of unleavened bread unto the LORD: seven days ye must eat unleavened bread. In the first day ye shall have an holy convocation: ye shall do no servile work therein. But ye shall offer an offering made by fire unto the LORD seven days: in the seventh day *is* an holy convocation: ye shall do no servile work *therein*.". Exodus 12:15-20 says, "Seven days shall ye eat unleavened bread; even the first day ye shall put away leaven out of your houses: for whosoever eateth leavened bread from the first day until the seventh day, that soul shall be cut off from Israel. And in the first day *there shall* be an holy convocation, and in the seventh day there shall be an holy convocation to you; no manner of work shall be done in them, save *that* which every man must eat, that only may be done of you. And ye shall observe *the feast of* unleavened bread; for in this selfsame day have I brought your armies out of the land of Egypt: therefore shall ye observe this day in your generations by an ordinance for ever. In the first *month,* on the fourteenth day of the month at even, ye shall eat unleavened bread, until the one and twentieth day of the month at even. Seven days shall there be no leaven found in your houses: for whosoever eateth that which is leavened, even that soul shall be cut off from the congregation of Israel, whether he be a stranger, or born in the land. Ye shall eat nothing leavened; in all your habitations shall ye eat unleavened bread.". Alleluia and praise the LORD. Amen and Amen.

Exodus12:33-39 explains the practical reasons why the Israelites could not make or eat leavened bread, namely because they were in too much of a haste to make bread with leaven in it during the initial exodus. Exodus 12:33-39 says, "And the Egyptians were urgent upon the people, that they might send them out of the land in haste; for they said, We *be* all dead *men*. And the people took their dough before it was leavened, their kneadingtroughs being bound up in their clothes upon their shoulders. And the children of Israel did according to the word of Moses; and they borrowed of the Egyptians jewels of silver, and jewels of gold, and raiment: And the LORD gave the people favour in the sight of the Egyptians, so that they lent unto them *such things as they required*. And they spoiled the Egyptians. And the children of Israel journeyed from Rameses to Succoth, about six hundred thousand on foot *that were* men, beside children. And a mixed multitude went up also with them; and flocks, and herds, *even* very much cattle. And they baked unleavened cakes of the dough which they brought forth out of Egypt, for it was not leavened; because they were thrust out of Egypt, and could not tarry, neither had they prepared for themselves any victual.". Exodus 12:38 is interesting in that it mentions a "...mixed multitude..." going with them. This would indicate that among the Israelites were some born of "...mixed..." descent as well; the Hebrew word for mixed is 'ereb, from the root word 'arab, Strong's numbers 6154 and 6148, respectively. This is partly the history of Israel and its relationship with the world, as well as Jesus Christ of Nazareth dying on the cross for the forgiveness of the sins of Israel, but for the whole world also, spilling His Holy and righteous blood on the cross at Passover in 31 A.D. (John 3:16). He was buried and the third day Jesus arose to give us the hope and promise of eternal life in His Holy name. The reality is that the descendants of Israel have always been amongst other nations and tribes of the earth, and although called to be separate and apart, we are still in the world (John 15:19, 1 John 2:15). This is why it is all the more important to know the truth of the Holy Bible and follow it; so that we do not become confused by the foreign customs, "gods" and idols of this world. That is, we need to remember the Exodus example message, that foreshadows and continues with Jesus Christ of Nazareth. We are called out of this world and its ways (2 Cor. 6:17, Rev. 18:4). We live in this world, in this life, but we need to cleanse ourselves of the idolatry and covetousness that comes along with it; that is, repent and believe in the true gospel of Jesus Christ of Nazareth and the kingdom of God, the Father, Almighty, through His Holy Spirit. Alleluia and praise the LORD. Amen and Amen.

Jesus' crucifixion, burial and resurrection the third day and the leaven of Jesus Christ of Nazareth; although there is nothing wrong with keeping the feast of unleavened bread today, we ought to put it into proper perspective. Jesus was resurrected in the middle of the feast of unleavened bread, if He was crucified on Passover, Wednesday, 14 Nisan in 31 A.D., and raised up Saturday afternoon sometime, 17 Nisan, three full days later, and before dawn on the first day of the week, 18 Nisan (Matt. 12:40). The days of unleavened bread would not have been finished until four days after His Saturday resurrection, after 21 Nisan in 31 A.D. (Ex. 12:18, Lev. 23:6). It is very possible, that Jesus was resurrected and ate with His disciples during the final few days of the feast of unleavened bread (Mark 16:14, Luke 24:29, 30). No doubt, He had visited the disciples during this time; the first day after His resurrection He visited them for certain, 18 Nisan in 31 A.D., and then, on at least a few more occasions afterwards, for about forty days (Mark 16:14, Luke 24:29, 30; John 20:19-23, 26-29; 21:1-14; Acts 1:1-8). After the forty days of His visitation upon His resurrection, He was taken and received into a cloud in heaven to sit at God, the Father's, right hand (Acts 1:9). And the outpouring of the Holy Spirit took place at Pentecost in 31 A.D., the feast of firstfruits, ten days after Jesus was taken up into a cloud in heaven (Acts 2:1-21). The feast of Pentecost and Jesus' relationship with it will be spoken of in greater detail in the next chapter. The days of unleavened bread can be a time for reflection and removing of "...old leaven..." from our life, the leaven of lies, and unforgiveness, etc. (1 Cor. 5:7, 8). As Jesus desires us to be a new creature in Him, He desires to renew us and give us life and life more abundantly (John 10:10). This is the great gift that we have in the offering of life, Jesus gave to us in His Holy name. Jesus Christ of Nazareth gave us forgiveness for our sins on the cross, He died on the cross, spilling His Holy and righteous blood for us. He was buried and He arose three days later for our hope and promise of eternal life in His Holy name. Alleluia and praise the LORD. Amen and Amen. There is a command to keep the feast of unleavened bread in the New Testament. 1 Corinthians 5:7 and 8 say, "Purge out therefore the old leaven, that ye may be a new lump, as ye are unleavened. For even Christ our Passover is sacrificed for us: Therefore let us keep the feast, not with old leaven, neither with the leaven of malice and wickedness; but with the unleavened *bread* of sincerity and truth.". Jesus is the truth, and the "...truth shall make you free." (John 8:32, 14:6). Last, the writers of the epistles of the New Testament, said that it is better to obey God then to keep the commandments of men (Acts 5:29). So with all of this information, so far, and in the remainder of this book, keep in mind your relationship with your Creator, God, the Father, Almighty and Jesus Christ of Nazareth, God's only begotten Son, through His Holy Spirit, first and foremost. Alleluia and praise the LORD. Amen and Amen.

Firstfruits and Jesus

Leviticus 23:9-14 says, "And the LORD spake unto Moses, saying, Speak unto the children of Israel, and say unto them, When ye be come into the land which I give unto you, and shall reap the harvest thereof, then ye shall bring a sheaf of the firstfruits of your harvest unto the priest: And he shall wave the sheaf before the LORD, to be accepted for you: on the morrow after the sabbath the priest shall wave it. And ye shall offer that day when ye wave the sheaf an he lamb without blemish of the first year for a burnt offering unto the LORD. And the meat offering thereof *shall be* two tenth deals of fine flour mingled with oil, an offering made by fire unto the LORD *for* a sweet savour: and the drink offering thereof *shall be* of wine, the fourth *part* of an hin. And ye shall eat neither bread, nor parched corn, nor green ears, until the selfsame day that ye have brought an offering unto your God: *it shall be* a statute for ever throughout your generations in all your dwellings.". This is likely the first day, after the first Sabbath, after Passover; this would always be on the first day of the week, on a Sunday. This is why Pentecost, seven weeks later is always on a Sunday (Lev. 23:15-22). The sheaf, likely of wheat, that is waved can be seen in Jesus Christ of Nazareth, after His resurrection Saturday; with the angel of the LORD at the tomb Sunday morning, and with Jesus revealing, "waving", Himself to His disciples, during the first day of the week, Sunday, and for forty days afterward (Matt. 28:2-10, 16-20). Jesus is the first of the firstfruits of God, and His disciples with the saints are the firstfruits of God (Ex. 29:13, Rom. 8:23, 1 Cor. 15:23, Jam. 1:18). The continuation of this day is concluded at the "...feast of weeks...", also known as Pentecost, as mentioned above briefly and in the next chapter (Ex. 34:22, Lev. 23:15-22). After Jesus' resurrection and ascension, this was concluded with the outpouring of the Holy Spirit at Pentecost in 31 A.D. (Acts 2:1-21). More will be spoken of about the feast of Pentecost in the next chapter. Alleluia and praise the LORD. Amen and Amen.

Conclusion

Amongst scholars, as of the date of writing this book in 2019 A.D.; it seems there is some disagreement of when Passover is, Jesus' crucifixion day, and the first day of the feast of unleavened bread (Mark 14:1). I think Jesus and the disciples celebrated the proper Passover the evening of the Passover, mentioned in the Old Testament, 14 Nisan, Tuesday evening in 31 A.D. (Lev. 23:5). That was the same Biblical calendar evening, 14 Nisan, during the Exodus from Egypt, that the destroyer was to come just hours later to pass over the houses of the Israelites and destroy the first born children of Egypt (Ex. 12:23). For some reason, it seems that the Jews had started celebrating the Passover during the first day of unleavened bread, either the evening after the proper Passover, the evening beginning 15th Nisan, the first day of unleavened bread, a Sabbath, a high day, or the evening after that, ending the first day of Unleavened bread, the end of 15 Nisan (Lev. 23:6, 7; John 19:31). There is some indication of this during Jesus' betrayal and judgement, as they did not desire to crucify Jesus on what the authorities considered the Passover (Matt 26:5). So this may be the confusion of what year, and day, Jesus was crucified, because traditionally people consider the Passover to have been eaten on the Wednesday or Thursday evening, which very well may have been the case for the Jews. But Jesus ate the true Passover with His disciples before that evening (John 12:1, 2). He and His disciples ate the Passover, likely Tuesday evening, He was betrayed Tuesday night, the beginning of 14 Nisan, and crucified Wednesday, the day of 14th Nisan, Passover day, in 31 A.D.. John considered six days before the Passover to be the day before Jesus' triumphal entry into Jerusalem, the Sunday before the crucifixion. That would mean Jesus' feet were anointed for His burial at the house by a woman, likely Saturday evening, 10 Nisan in 31 A.D. (John 12:1-7, 12). But he may have been referring to the traditional "Jewish" celebration of Passover, not the true Passover celebrated by Jesus' and His disciples according to the Law of Moses (Lev. 23:5). God knows. To view more detail on Jesus' crucifixion week according to this interpretation, see appendix D. To God be the glory in the truth of all of these things, and most important, is to remember that Jesus Christ of Nazareth, did indeed come to earth. He was conceived by the Holy Spirit in the virgin, Mary, espoused to Joseph. He was born of the virgin, Mary, espoused to Joseph and He was raised a child of Israel, of the tribe of Judah, with brothers and sisters (Matt. 1:18-25, 13:55, 56; Luke 2:41-52, Rev. 5:5). He started His ministry in the fall of 27 A.D., at about the age of thirty, and He ministered for three and a half years. He gave up His life for all of us on the cross, dying for the forgiveness of our sins on the cross at Passover in 31 A.D.. He was buried and the third day He arose to give us the hope and promise of eternal life in His Holy name. Alleluia and praise the LORD. Amen and Amen.

Speaking of the hour of "...the power of darkness...", which Jesus endured during His betrayal, trial and crucifixion; in reference to the "Great Tribulation", Jesus prophesied of, and the ten kings, spoken of in the book of Revelation and referenced similarly by the prophet Daniel (Dan. 2:41-45, Luke 22:53, Rev. 17:12-14). This could refer to Judas' betrayal of Jesus, His disciples scattering, and Peter's denial of being a disciple of Jesus Christ of Nazareth (Matt. 26:14-16, Mark 14:50, Luke 22:54-62). Jesus was literally blind folded and smote in the face and asked to prophecy, who hit him (Luke 22:63, 64). He said He would be set at nought, and He was during His trial (Mark 9:12). That is, His accusers did not believe He was whom He said He was, the Son of God (Matt. 26:59-66). Nevertheless, even in the midst of Jesus' darkest hour, He mentions in the gospel according to John, that God, the Father, is with Him (John 16:32). John mentions very similarly at the beginning of his account of the gospel of Jesus Christ of Nazareth, that "...the light shineth in darkness; and the darkness comprehended it not." (John 1:5). John even writes about Jesus, "He was in the world, and the world was made by him, and the world knew him not." (John 1:10). But finally after He gave up the Holy Ghost on the cross, and the earthquake took place, a centurion and those with the centurion, did say of Jesus Christ of Nazareth, "...Truly this was the Son of God." (Matt. 27:54). Alleluia and praise the LORD. Amen and Amen. This also reflects Jesus, as the Passover Lamb, when the destroyer passed over the houses of the Israelites whom had the lamb's blood on their door posts and lintel (Ex. 12:23). So, we ought to apply the blood of Jesus Christ of Nazareth to our life to receive eternal life in His Holy name. Alleluia and praise the LORD. Amen and Amen. Jesus was indeed three days and three nights in the grave, using the sign of Jonah (Matt. 12:40). Isaiah 26:19 says, "Thy dead *men* shall live, *together with* my dead body shall they arise. Awake and sing, ye that dwell in dust: for thy dew *is as* the dew of herbs, and the earth shall cast out the dead.". This speaks of the promise of the resurrection at the last day, which will be spoken of in greater detail in chapter six. However, we are called to dwell in Christ's life, death and resurrection; not in the life, death and resurrection of this world (John 14:27, 2 Cor. 7:9-11). In the next chapter, I will speak about the feast of Pentecost, and the Holy Spirit that God, the Father, has given to all whom believe in Jesus Christ of Nazareth, His only begotten Son. Alleluia and praise the LORD. Amen and Amen. Read on to learn more.

Discussion: Passover

"By the which will we are sanctified through the offering
of the body of Jesus Christ once *for all*."
- Hebrews 10:10

Jesus Christ of Nazareth said on the cross, "...My God, my God, why hast thou forsaken me?" (Matt. 27:46). I have addressed this question in a few places in my writing, but I will speak of it from a different perspective here. Jesus cast out a devil from a boy that was dumb and deaf (Mark 9:25). I heard once, that Satan is very intelligent, but if we know somebody by their fruits, then how could Satan be intelligent (Matt. 7:16)? Nevertheless, similar to this boy, Jesus seems to have manifested the complete separation from God by taking all of our sin upon Himself on the cross (Matt. 27:46). The apostle, Paul, even said God made Jesus to be sin who knew no sin (2 Cor. 5:21). The point is, that Jesus Christ of Nazareth suffered much in order for us to be saved. He was crowned with a crown of thorns (Matt. 27:29, Mark 15:17, John 19:1). And the apostle, Paul, had a thorn in the flesh, the messenger of Satan to humble him, but God said, "My grace is sufficient for thee..." (2 Cor. 12:7-9). In weakness, God's strength is perfected, and of course this goes for any of us, including our Saviour Jesus Christ of Nazareth, whose weakness was an earthly death on the cross for the forgiveness of our sins (2 Cor. 12:9). Nevertheless, in both the New and Old Testament, I have come across at least a few of what some may consider, "contradictions", between various disciples accounts of how Jesus lived His life, and how these disciples recorded them either first hand or by eyewitness account (Luke 1:1-4). I have done some thought about all of this, and I think the crown of thorns describes this whole situation well. The Holy Bible of God, and life in some respects can seem to be a crown of thorns, when we are persecuted, commit sin and are punished, when we are struggling with understanding of what God is doing, and saying through His Word, the Holy Bible and how He desires us to live this life (Job 31:35, 36). But ultimately, we must place our trust in the true God, the living God, through Jesus Christ of Nazareth. Whom died on the cross for the forgiveness of our sins at Passover in 31 A.D., shedding His

Holy and righteous blood on the cross. He was buried and the third day He arose again to give us the hope and promise of eternal life in His Holy name. Alleluia and praise the LORD. The apostle, Paul, speaks of the love of Christ that passes knowledge, and the peace of God that passes understanding (Eph. 3:19, Phil. 4:7). So just like our failures in sin, which bring us to death, so to through Jesus Christ of Nazareth, are we redeemed to our Creator, God, the Father, through His only begotten Son, Jesus Christ of Nazareth. Alleluia and praise the LORD. And He has given us of His Holy Spirit to dwell in and with us forever (1 John 4:13). Jesus Christ of Nazareth and God, the Father, through His Holy Spirit are with us forever (Matt. 28:20). Alleluia and praise the LORD. Amen and Amen. When reading through this section's discussions, consider your relationship with your Creator, in Christ Jesus of Nazareth; and how He desires you to live out the remainder of your life here on earth, and in the "world to come", eternal life. Alleluia and praise the LORD. Amen and Amen.

Discussion Questions

1. What is the appropriate age to learn the deeper things of God?

    _____

    _____

    _____

2. What about nature? Can we learn from God's creation outside of the Bible and the Holy Spirit working through other people?

    _____

    _____

    _____

3. Can we learn from the memories and experiences of our ancestors whom have passed before us?

    _____

    _____

    _____

CHAPTER 4

Pentecost

"…I will pour out my spirit upon all flesh…"
- Joel 2:28

Introduction

Three times in a year all "…menchildren…" are called to present ourselves before the Lord God, that is, at the feast of Unleavened bread, the feast of Pentecost, and the feast of Tabernacles (Ex. 23:14-17, 34:23; Deut. 16:16). The feast of harvest, the feast of weeks, and the feast of Pentecost, are all the same feast; known as Pentecost, in the New Testament (Ex. 23:16, 34:22; Acts 2:1). This chapter will speak about Pentecost, according to the Old Testament commandments, along with the similitude in keeping the feast, that points to the greater plan of God for all of mankind. Alleluia and praise the LORD. Amen and Amen. Read on to learn more.

Old Testament

Leviticus 23:15-21 says, "And ye shall count unto you from the morrow after the sabbath, from the day that ye brought the sheaf of the wave offering; seven Sabbaths shall be complete: Even unto the morrow after the seventh sabbath shall ye number fifty days; and ye shall offer a new meat offering unto the LORD. Ye shall bring out of your habitations two wave loaves of two tenth deals; they shall be of fine flour; they shall be baken with leaven; *they are* the firstfruits unto the LORD. And ye shall offer with the bread seven lambs without blemish of the first year, and one young bullock, and two rams: they shall be *for* a burnt offering unto the LORD, with their meat offering, and their drink offerings, *even* an offering made by fire, of sweet savour unto the LORD. Then ye shall sacrifice one kid of the goats for a sin offering, and two lambs of the first year for a sacrifice of peace offerings. And the priest shall wave them with the bread of the firstfruits *for* a wave offering before the LORD, with the two lambs: they shall be holy to the LORD for the priest. And ye shall proclaim on the selfsame day, *that* it may be an holy convocation unto you: ye shall do no servile work *therein: it shall be* a statute for ever in all your dwellings throughout your generations.". Alleluia and praise the LORD. Amen and Amen.

It could be suggested that the feast of weeks is related to the days of unleavened bread, after a sabbath, in the same week of the feast of unleavened bread (Lev. 23:9-14). Or that it may be related to the seven weeks working towards Pentecost (Acts 2:1). The fact of the matter is, that there is no shadow of a doubt in my mind, that scripture indicates that the feast of harvest, is the feast of weeks, and is the Pentecost day of the New Testament (Ex. 23:16, 34:22; Acts 2:1). These are all the same feast, on the same day, the first day, after the seventh Sabbath, after Passover (Lev. 23:15, 16). Numbers 28:26 confirms "...after your weeks *be out*..."; likely meaning after the seven weeks have passed (Num. 28:26-31). Exodus 34:22 very clearly separates the feast of weeks from the feast of unleavened bread; and the feast of weeks, and the feast of harvest are the same as Pentecost, as mentioned, and will always be on the first day of the week, Sunday (Ex. 23:16, 34:22; Acts 2:1). It is only in Leviticus 23 that the interpretation could cause questioning, needing to discern how to separate Leviticus 23:9-14 and Leviticus 23:15-21. The argument would be; which feast or feasts are these two sets of verses related to, Pentecost or the feast of unleavened bread, or both (Lev. 23:4-8, 15-21, Acts 2:1). The last section of the previous chapter covered the day of the "...wave..." of the sheaf, the first day, after the first sabbath, after Passover, mentioned in Leviticus 23:9-14, the first day of the week, Sunday, when Jesus revealed Himself to His disciples (Matt. 28). Then, seven weeks later we have the feast of weeks, Pentecost, and the point of the feast of weeks in the Old Testament was to bring the firstfruits of the harvest to the LORD (Lev. 23:17, 20; Acts 2:1). Although I am not an expert, in growing in climates similar to Israel proper; it seems that cereal grains can be sown in the fall, and grown throughout winter, in these warmer climates. This would enable a spring harvest for these cereal crops, with a sheaf of the firstfruits given to the priest to "... wave the sheaf...", that would likely be of wheat, as said in the previous chapter (Lev. 23:10, 11). Also, there is mention of preparing and giving firstfruits of corn, bread, oil and wine (Lev. 2:14-16, 23:17; Num. 18:12). These all need preparing, that is, harvesting, processing and either leavening and baking, or fermenting and otherwise. The point here is, that the time between the initial harvest and the "... wave [of] the sheaf...", in and around the beginning of the Ecclesiastical Hebrew calendar year, Nisan/ Abib, until the feast of weeks, would be sufficient time to do all the preparing necessary to offer up these firstfruits of the harvest to the LORD, about seven weeks later, in the third month of the Hebrew calendar (Lev. 23:9-21, Deut. 16:1-12). That being said, the oil and wine may have been the firstfruits of the previous year's harvest. God knows. Alleluia and praise the LORD. Amen and Amen.

The feast of harvest or feast of weeks, also known as Pentecost in the New Testament, is one of the three occasions in the year, that we are called to present ourselves before the Lord God (Ex. 23:14-17, Deut. 16:16, Acts 2:1). The two other feasts are, as mentioned earlier, the feast of unleavened bread, in the first month of the Hebrew calendar year, and the feast of ingathering, in the seventh month of the Hebrew year, also known as the feast of tabernacles (Lev. 23:6-8, 33-44). An aside; the meat offering is seasoned with salt, and in the New Testament we are called to be the salt of the earth (Lev. 2:12, 13; Matt. 5:13). In the Old Testament, Israel is considered the firstfruits of God. Jeremiah 2:3 says, "Israel *was* holiness unto the LORD, *and* the firstfruits of his increase: all that devour him shall offend; evil shall come upon them, saith the LORD.". This is the beginning of the sign of the similitude of the feast of weeks, like the similitudes the other feasts of the LORD represent, a "...shadow of things to come..." (Col. 2:17). Alleluia and praise the LORD. Amen and Amen.

New Testament

As mentioned in the previous section, the Holy day of, the feast of weeks, is a sign; that God calls us, His spiritually begotten children, to be His firstfruits (John 1:12, 13; Rom. 8:23). And Jesus Christ of

Nazareth is the first of the firstfruits of God; mentioned in the last section of the last chapter, the sheaf that is waved (Lev. 23:10, 11; 1 Cor. 15:20). Then, Jesus' promise of the Holy Spirit was fulfilled at Pentecost, fifty days after His resurrection, and seven weeks after His first appearance to His disciples after His resurrection (Acts 1:1-9). Acts 2:1-4 says, "And when the day of Pentecost was fully come, they were all with one accord in one place. And suddenly there came a sound from heaven as of a rushing mighty wind, and it filled all the house where they were sitting. And there appeared unto them cloven tongues like as of fire, and it sat upon each of them. And they were all filled with the Holy Ghost, and began to speak with other tongues, as the Spirit gave them utterance.". The apostle, Paul, speaks about the law being written in our hearts, and the other New Testament writers of the epistles also confirm the Holy Spirit's significance in our relationship with God, the Father, and Jesus Christ of Nazareth, along with our fellowship with the body of Christ, the church of God in this world, and with this world, in general. The apostle, Paul, speaks of the gentiles as being a law unto themselves, not knowing the law, but doing by nature, what is written in the law (Rom. 2:14, 15). Nevertheless, we are also firstfruits with the elect of God (Rev. 14:4). Fellowcitizens with the saints (Eph. 2:19-22). This happens when, as the Bible says of Jesus Christ of Nazareth, "...as many as received him, to them gave he power to become the sons of God, even to them that believe on his name: Which were born, not of blood, nor of the will of the flesh, nor of the will of man, but of God." (John 1:12, 13). We are begotten children of God, through faith in, and belief on our Saviour, Jesus Christ of Nazareth (Eph. 2:8, 9). Jesus Christ of Nazareth, was born into this world, conceived by the Holy Spirit in and born of the virgin, Mary, espoused to Joseph (Matt. 1:18-25). He was raised, a child of Israel, of the tribe of Judah and had brothers and sisters (Matt. 13:55, 56; Luke 2:41-52, Rev. 5:5). He began His earthly ministry, at about the age of thirty, in the fall of 27 A.D.; and He healed, forgave, and did other miracles for about three and a half years (Luke 3:23). And at Passover in 31 A.D., He gave His life for us, dying on the cross for the forgiveness of our sins, shedding His Holy and righteous blood. He was buried and the third day He arose to give us the hope and promise of eternal life in His Holy name. Alleluia and praise the LORD. Amen and Amen.

Messianic Age and the kingdom of God living in us

Ezekiel 20:39-41 says, "As for you, O house of Israel, thus saith the Lord GOD; Go ye, serve ye every one his idols, and hereafter *also,* if ye will not hearken unto me: but pollute ye my holy name no more with your gifts, and with your idols. For in mine holy mountain, in the mountain of the height of Israel, saith the Lord GOD, there shall all of the house of Israel, all of them in the land, serve me: there will I accept them, and there will I require your offerings, and the firstfruits of your oblations, with all your holy things. I will accept you with your sweet savour, when I bring you out from the people, and gather you out of the countries wherein ye have been scattered; and I will be sanctified in you before the heathen.". This is prophetic of the "Messianic Age", but has also taken place, especially in the 20th century, with Israel becoming a modern nation state in 1948, recognized by the United Nations of this world. In the "Messianic age", the firstfruits are for the priests. Ezekiel 44:30 says, "And the first of all the firstfruits of all *things,* and every oblation of all, of every *sort* of your oblations, shall be the priest's: ye shall also give unto the priest the first of your dough, that he may cause the blessing to rest in thine house.". Ezekiel 48:14 says regarding the priests' allotted land, "And they shall not sell of it, neither exchange, nor alienate the firstfruits of the land: for it is holy unto the LORD.". But we must not forget about the promise of the Holy Spirit in all of this (John 14:16-18). Jesus Christ of

Nazareth made a promise, that after His resurrection, and ascension to God, the Father, in heaven, that He would send His Holy Spirit, to be with us and in us forever, even to the end of this world (Matt. 28:19, 20; John 14:16-18). This is that promise we have in the feast of Pentecost; that God has given us, His only begotten Son, Jesus Christ of Nazareth, to be with us forever. And that He will be with us always, even until the end of the world (Matt. 28:19, 20). Alleluia and praise the LORD. Amen and Amen. See appendix E for more details of the role of the church in the "Messianic Age".

Conclusion

Deuteronomy 30:14 says, "...the word *is* very nigh unto thee, in thy mouth, and in thy heart, that thou mayest do it.". The apostle, Paul, reminds us of this, writing, "But what saith it? The word is very nigh thee, *even* in thy mouth, and in thy heart..." (Rom. 10:8). The Holy Bible speaks of the "...sacrifice of praise..." (Jer. 33:11). And Jesus said, "...the hour cometh, and now is, when the true worshippers shall worship the Father in spirit and in truth..." (Ps. 40:7, 8; John 4:23). So our reality, ultimately, ought to be in the life, death on the cross for the forgiveness of our sins, and the resurrection three days later, of Jesus Christ of Nazareth, for our hope and promise of eternal life in His Holy name. Alleluia and praise the LORD. Amen and Amen. The next chapter will speak about the two fall Holy days, the feast of trumpets and the Day of Atonement; these lead to the final feast, the feast of tabernacles, including the last great day, that will be spoken of in chapter six of this book. Read on to learn more. Alleluia and praise the LORD. Amen and Amen.

Discussion: Firstfruits

> "...freely ye have received, freely give."
> - Matthew 10:8

The Holy Bible speaks of giving our firstfruits to God, tithing and being a cheerful giver (Ex. 23:19, Lev. 27:30, 2 Cor. 9:7). The apostle, Paul, spoke of husbandman, that labour, being first partaker of the fruits (2 Tim. 2:6). I suppose this could be his way of encouraging a savings of some sorts. For practical reasons probably, because God desired the church of God, and the congregation to have a certain degree of independence from the governing system of that time, and whatever social welfare programs they had. The same is still relevant for us today. Of course, financial investment institutions teach to save the first ten percent for ourselves. But no matter, as 1 Chronicles 29:14 says of God, "...all things *come* of thee, and of thine own have we given thee.". That is, the reality is, that all our money, possessions, lands, etc., ultimately belong to the Creator, God, the Father, Almighty, whom created all things (John 1:3, Rev. 4:11). He has given us the earth, and He has given it to us to inhabit, and even have dominion over, but this requires obedience to Him, first and foremost (Gen. 1:28). And more importantly, Jesus Christ of Nazareth said of Himself that "...All power is given unto me in heaven and in earth." (Matt. 28:18). So the reality is, that everything we have, do and see, come from our Creator, in the name of His only begotten Son, Jesus Christ of Nazareth, whom died on the cross for the forgiveness of our sins at Passover in 31 A.D., shedding His Holy and righteous blood for us. He was buried and on the third day He arose to give us the hope and promise of eternal life in His Holy name. Alleluia and praise the LORD. Amen and Amen. Jesus said "...Make to yourselves friends of the mammon of unrighteousness; that, when ye fail, they may receive you into everlasting habitations." (Luke 16:9). Two examples come to mind when thinking about what Jesus is saying, the first is that He miraculously had a coin appear in the mouth of a fish for Peter to use to pay the tribute to the tribute money collector (Matt. 17:24-27). And the widow's mite, is the second example, whom Jesus said, cast more into the treasury out of her penury, than all that the rich men had cast in out of there abundance (Mark 12:41-44). So again, this is the reality we have in Jesus Christ of Nazareth; that He is a miracle worker, and that giving when we think we have next to nothing, is a much greater gift then giving some, out of abundance. This is why Jesus said, "Blessed are the poor in spirit…" (Matt. 5:3). And why He spoke of faith as a mustard seed (Matt. 17:20). Alleluia and praise the LORD. Amen and Amen.

Discussion Questions

1. The Bible speaks in many places of the traps, snares and pits that the enemy creates for us. What can you do to avoid these pitfalls in life? What does the Bible say about those who create these pits?

2. What is required of us to be teachers of God's truth? (Hint: Psalm 51:11-13)

3. Who is the ultimate teacher?

CHAPTER 5

Feast of Trumpets and
Day of Atonement

"Moreover by them is thy servant warned: and in keeping of them there is great reward."
- Psalm 19:11

Introduction

There are two Holy days preceding the fall feast of Tabernacles; they are the feast of Trumpets and the Day of Atonement (Lev. 23:24-32). It has been said, prophetically, they are related to the announcement of the outset of the "Messianic age" and Christ's "second coming" (Isa. 27:13).[13] The feast of Tabernacles being the culmination of these fall Holy days; representing the last 1000 years of God's rule in the present 7000 year plan of God, with His creation here on earth, through the guidance of His Holy Spirit, in Jesus Christ of Nazareth, God's only begotten Son, with God, the Father, and the saints, likely in spirit form (Ps. 90:4, 104:4; 2 Pet. 3:8). This is before the judgement and the "...new heavens and a new earth..." to come, that will be spoken of in the next chapter (2 Pet. 3:13, Rev. 20:11-15, 21:1-8). In this chapter, I will go into greater detail of the references to the feast of Trumpets and the Day of Atonement, in both the Old Testament and New; and I will speak about the various purposes for each of these feasts, as a memorial, their prophetic significance in Jesus Christ of Nazareth's life and as a shadow of things to come (Col. 2:16, 17; Heb. 10:1). I will also speak about the various types of offerings that can be given during the feasts, and in our everyday life, to live the give way of life. Alleluia and praise the LORD. Amen and Amen. Read on to learn more.

Feast of Trumpets

Leviticus 23:24 and 25 say, "Speak unto the children of Israel, saying, In the seventh month, in the first *day* of the month, shall ye have a sabbath, a memorial of blowing of trumpets, an holy convocation. Ye shall do no servile work *therein:* but ye shall offer an offering made by fire unto the LORD.". Numbers 29:1-6 says, "And in the seventh month, on the first *day* of the month, ye shall have an holy convocation; ye shall do no servile work: it is a day of blowing the trumpets unto you. And ye shall offer a burnt offering for a sweet savour unto the LORD; one young bullock, one ram, *and* seven lambs

---

[13] https://www.jewishvoice.org/read/blog/rosh-hashanah-jewish-new-year, retrieved 25/04/2022

of the first year without blemish: And their meat offering *shall be of* flour mingled with oil, three tenth deals for a bullock, *and* two tenth deals for a ram, And one tenth deal for one lamb, throughout the seven lambs: And one kid of the goats *for* a sin offering, to make an atonement for you: Beside the burnt offering of the month, and his meat offering, and the daily burnt offering, and his meat offering, and their drink offerings, according unto their manner, for a sweet savour, a sacrifice made by fire unto the LORD.". This Holy day is the first of the fall Holydays and likely has something to do with marking the beginning of the fall Holy days by the blowing of the trumpets. It also has been said to be the beginning of the ten days of reflection culminating with the Day of Atonement, according to Jewish authorities.[14] This would make sense because if the sins of ancient Israel were to be atoned for on the Day of Atonement, no doubt, it would be a good idea to warn the people of the coming, Day of Atonement, so that people could repent and prepare for the offering that was to be given (Lev. 23:27-32). Nevertheless, in Jesus Christ of Nazareth, we have the New Covenant on the cross at Passover in 31 A.D., and Jesus' life giving offering to look to always, for our hope and forgiveness of our sins. Putting these feast days in the light of the life of Jesus Christ of Nazareth, brings a renewed purpose and meaning to these fall Holy days, even all of the Leviticus 23 Holy days. Alleluia and praise the LORD. Amen and Amen.

There has been a suggestion that Jesus was born on the feast of trumpets, see appendices B and F for details and references, respectively.[15] I would suggest it is the likely Holyday, if at all, for Jesus Christ of Nazareth's birth, 1 Ethanim/Tishri in 4 B.C. (Lev. 23:24, Luke 2:1-20). Hosea 8:1 says, "*Set the trumpet to thy mouth, He shall come* as an eagle against the house of the LORD, because they have transgressed my covenant, and trespassed against my law.". The eagle is often associated with the Roman Empire, and Joseph and Mary had to go to Bethlehem to pay taxes just as Jesus was to be born (Luke 2:1-5). Luke 2:6-20 says, "And so it was, that, while they were there, the days were accomplished that she should be delivered. And she brought forth her firstborn son, and wrapped him in swaddling clothes, and laid him in a manger; because there was no room for them in the inn. And there were in the same country shepherds abiding in the field, keeping watch over their flock by night. And, lo, the angel of the Lord came upon them, and the glory of the Lord shone round about them: and they were sore afraid. And the angel said unto them, Fear not: for, behold, I bring you good tidings of great joy, which shall be to all people. For unto you is born this day in the city of David a Saviour, which is Christ the Lord. And this *shall be* a sign unto you; Ye shall find the babe wrapped in swaddling clothes, lying in a manger. And suddenly there was with the angel a multitude of the heavenly host praising God, and saying, Glory to God in the highest, and on earth peace, good will toward men. And it came to pass, as the angels were gone away from them into heaven, the shepherds said one to another, Let us now go even unto Bethlehem, and see this thing which is come to pass, which the Lord hath made known unto us. And they came with haste, and found Mary, and Joseph, and the babe lying in a manger. And when they had seen *it,* they made known abroad the saying which was told them concerning this child. And all they that heard *it* wondered at those things which were told them by the shepherds. But Mary kept all these things, and pondered *them* in her heart. And the shepherds returned, glorifying and praising God for all the things that they had heard and seen, as it was told unto them.". Ezekiel 36:38 may give some sign of Jesus being born on a Holyday, it says, "As the holy flock, as the flock of Jerusalem in her solemn feasts…". Isaiah 58:1 says, "Cry aloud, spare

---

[14] https://www.myjewishlearning.com/article/the-ten-days-of-repentance/, retrieved 25/04/2022

[15] https://www.facebook.com/joeamaralpublic/posts/today-is-tishri-1-on-the-hebrew-calendar-its-known-as-rosh-hashanah-and-the-jewi/1712097898836485/, retrieved 15/04/2022

not, lift up thy voice like a trumpet, and shew my people their transgression, and the house of Jacob their sins.". These Old Testament prophecies are, no doubt, related to the prophecy of Jesus' birth and life ministry; albeit, He could not speak as a baby born at this time, but the shepherds did a great job of it (John 5:39). This may have also been around the time of the year when the "...wise men..." visited Jesus, when He was about two years old, before He and His parents fled into Egypt away from king Herod, in late 2 B.C. (Matt. 2:1-18). John the Baptist certainly fulfilled this trumpeting in his ministry, in the spirit of Elijah, telling the people to repent and prepare the way of the Lord (Matt. 3:1-3). The feast of Trumpets leads up to the Day of Atonement, ten days later at 10 Ethanim/Tishri, which is the day the sins of the people were atoned for in the Old Testament covenant (Lev. 23:26-32). But now with Jesus, we always have salvation and forgiveness, as we receive Him each day, through God's Holy Spirit, in Christ Jesus of Nazareth's Holy name by Jesus' Holy and righteous blood spilt on the cross for the forgiveness of our sins at Passover in 31 A.D.. He died on the cross, He was buried and the third day He arose to give us the hope and promise of eternal life in His Holy name. Alleluia and praise the LORD. Amen and Amen.

In the "...time of the end...", pre-great tribulation trumpet warnings are mentioned in the book of Joel and elsewhere in the Holy Bible, as of the date of writing this book in 2019 A.D. (Dan. 12:9). Joel 2:1 says, "Blow ye the trumpet in Zion, and sound an alarm in my holy mountain: let all the inhabitants of the land tremble: for the day of the LORD cometh, for *it is* nigh at hand.". Joel 2:15 also speaks of this blowing of the trumpet which prophecies of God's redemption of His people and His pouring out of His Holy Spirit on all flesh, etc., which did indeed happen at Pentecost in 31 A.D., but continues and will continue on, today and into the future (Joel 2:28, Acts 2:1-21). But we must still be aware, that there may very well be a short time, about three and a half years, ahead, just before the "Messianic Age", that is known as the "...time of Jacob's trouble..." and the "Great Tribulation", as of the date of writing this book in 2019 A.D. (Jer. 30:7, Matt. 24). Matthew 24:31 says, "And he shall send his angels with a great sound of a trumpet, and they shall gather together his elect from the four winds, from one end of heaven to the other.". This is likely just after the "Great Tribulation", spoken of by Jesus in Matthew 24, but spiritually is already taking place and has been for thousands of years (Matt. 24:21). Isaiah 27:13 says similarly, "And it shall come to pass in that day, *that* the great trumpet shall be blown, and they shall come which were ready to perish in the land of Assyria, and the outcasts in the land of Egypt, and shall worship the LORD in the holy mount at Jerusalem.". This trumpet could very well mark the beginning of the "Messianic age", the 1000 years of Christ's rule with His saints (Rev. 20:4, 6). If this were the case, it is possible that the "Great Tribulation", I have mentioned earlier, would likely start sometime in the early spring, as it is likely three and one half years long (Dan. 12:7, Rev. 11:3). I am hesitant to even write this, as Jesus warns of setting dates for His coming again, but the reality is the signs may suggest these to be truthful, time will tell. Alleluia and praise the LORD. Amen and Amen.

The Holy days do point to yet to be fulfilled prophecy of earth and mankind's history on it; and in the past they have been very accurate, so there is no reason to believe otherwise today, or for things yet to come. The only thing I would not do, is give a specific date or year for these events to take place, as only God knows the truth of this information. Jesus said, "But of that day and hour knoweth no *man*, no, not the angels of heaven, but my Father only." (Matt. 24:36). This was repeated in a broader sense in the book of Acts, "...It is not for you to know the times or the seasons, which the Father has put in his own power." (Acts 1:7). The reality is, Christ could come back today, and if you understand His coming from a spiritual perspective, and you accept His offering and sacrifice for the forgiveness of your sins, He will come into your life today. This is the bigger picture of Jesus' coming again, that He is coming to live with us and in us and to give us life everlasting (John 14:16-18). His "second coming", may very well be at a different time for each person in this earth, as we develop in our relationship with Him and others and then pass on, awaiting our resurrection, judgement and hopefully life everlasting in Jesus Christ of Nazareth, and God, the Father's, everlasting kingdom, in the "…new heavens and a new earth…", with His Holy Spirit (2 Pet. 3:13, Rev. 21:1). A New Testament writer and apostle, Paul, wrote, "In a moment, in the twinkling of an eye, at the last trump: for the trumpet shall sound, and the dead shall be raised incorruptible, and we shall be changed." (1 Cor. 15:52). He is very general in writing this passage, because according to the book of Revelations there are two resurrections, the first for the saints, the "…firstfruits…", at the beginning of the "Messianic Age", and then the second resurrection of the "…general assembly…" and all of mankind at the "last great day" of judgement, at the end of the "Messianic Age" (Rom. 8:23, Heb. 12:23, Rev. 20:11-15). All this being said, there is, no doubt, specific times in earth's history, that God has set apart for certain events, that fulfill God's prophecies of His plans for us and the earth as a whole. And all of the Holy days are a "…shadow…" of these events, as I have been explaining (Col. 2:17). But in order to keep it simple, following Jesus Christ of Nazareth, the only begotten Son of God, and God, the Father, with His Holy Spirit in our daily life, ought to be first priority for any believer in God, the Father, Almighty through His only begotten Son, Jesus Christ of Nazareth. To God be the Glory, forever and ever. Alleluia and praise the LORD. Amen and Amen.

Day of Atonement

Leviticus 16:3-10 says, "Thus shall Aaron come into the holy *place:* with a young bullock for a sin offering, and a ram for a burnt offering. He shall put on the holy linen coat, and he shall have the linen breeches upon his flesh, and shall be girded with a linen girdle, and with the linen mitre shall he be attired: these *are* holy garments; therefore shall he wash his flesh in water, and *so* put them on. And he shall take of the congregation of the children of Israel two kids of the goats for a sin offering, and one ram for a burnt offering. And Aaron shall offer his bullock of the sin offering, which *is* for himself, and make an atonement for himself, and for his house. And he shall take the two goats, and present them before the LORD *at* the door of the tabernacle of the congregation. And Aaron shall cast lots upon the two goats; one lot for the LORD, and the other lot for the scapegoat. And Aaron shall bring the goat upon which the LORD's lot fell, and offer him *for* a sin offering. But the goat, on which the lot fell to be the scapegoat, shall be presented alive before the LORD, to make an atonement with him, *and* to let him go for a scapegoat into the wilderness.". Leviticus 16:29-34 says, "And *this* shall be a statute for ever unto you: *that* in the seventh month, on the tenth *day* of the month, ye shall afflict your souls, and do no work at all, *whether it be* one of your own country, or a stranger that sojourneth among you: For on that day shall *the priest* make an atonement for you, to cleanse you, *that* ye may be clean from all your sins before the LORD. It *shall be* a sabbath of rest unto you, and ye shall afflict your souls, by a statute for ever. And the priest, whom he shall anoint, and whom he shall consecrate to minister in the priest's office in his father's stead, shall make the atonement, and shall put on the linen clothes, *even* the holy garments: And he shall make an atonement for the holy sanctuary, and he shall make an atonement for the tabernacle of the congregation, and for the altar, and he shall make an atonement for the priests, and for the people of the congregation. And this shall be an everlasting statute unto you, to make an atonement for the children of Israel for all their sins once a year. And he did as the LORD commanded Moses.". Leviticus 23:27-32 says, "Also on the tenth *day* of this seventh month *there shall be* a day of atonement: it shall be an holy convocation unto you; and ye shall afflict your souls, and offer an offering made by fire unto the LORD. And ye shall do no work in that same day: for it *is* a day of atonement, to make an atonement for you before the LORD your God. For whatsoever soul *it be* that shall not be afflicted in that same day, he shall be cut off from among his people. And whatsoever soul it be that doeth any work in that same day, the same soul will I destroy from among his people. Ye shall do no manner of work: *it shall be* a statute for ever throughout your generations in all your dwellings. It *shall be* unto you a sabbath of rest, and ye shall afflict your souls: in the ninth *day* of the month at even, from even unto even, shall ye celebrate your sabbath.". Alleluia and praise the LORD. Amen and Amen.

This day can remind us of Jesus, as a very young child, after His 8th day circumcision, which would likely have been a day or so before the Day of Atonement in 4 B.C., if He was born on the first day of the seventh month (Lev. 12:1-3, Luke 2:21). He would have been prepared to be the atonement for God, the house of Israel, and for the whole world. About two years later, around the same time of year, in 2 B.C.; Jesus and His parents fled into Egypt to protect Jesus from evil king Herod, whom desired to kill the child (Matt. 2:13-15). Although He was not "sacrificed" physically on the Day of Atonement, the scapegoat is, no doubt, a sign of Jesus Christ of Nazareth's earthly life, before His crucifixion at Passover in 31 A.D.; as He and His parents were seemingly without a place to stay at His birth, near that time of year (Luke 2:7). Also, as said, He and His parents had to flee into Egypt two years after that, near that time of year in 2 B.C., and again, as will be mentioned in the next chapter, Jesus was taken into the wilderness after His baptism in 27 A.D., likely on the first day of the feast of Tabernacles, five days after the Day of Atonement (Lev. 23:34-43). It is incredible, the signs these Holy days are, of Jesus Christ of Nazareth, our Saviour's life, death on the cross for the forgiveness of our sins, burial and resurrection three days later, for a testimony to His Messiahship and for us to believe and have hope in. Understanding that Jesus Christ of Nazareth died on the cross for the forgiveness of our sins, our atonement with God, at Passover in 31 A.D., spilling His Holy and righteous blood, He was buried and He arose the third day for our hope and promise of eternal life in His Holy name; puts this day into better perspective for all believers. The apostle, Paul, said, "...can never with those sacrifices which they offered year by year continually make the comers thereunto perfect. ...we are sanctified through the offering of the body of Jesus Christ once for all." (Heb. 10:1, 10). Isaiah 58:8 says, "Then shall thy light break forth as the morning, and thine health shall spring forth speedily: and thy righteousness shall go before thee; the glory of the LORD shall be thy rereward.". The revelation of Jesus Christ of Nazareth in the scriptures; the Holy days, and in prophecy in general, including the New Testament witnesses of His life amongst us as Immanuel, are the testimonies we need to let our "...light break forth..." in this world, as a city set on a hill (Isa. 58:8, Matt. 1:23, 5:14). It is by the truth of Jesus Christ of Nazareth's life, sacrificial offering at Passover in 31 A.D. on the cross, His burial and His resurrection three days later; that the Day of Atonement is turned from a day of affliction to a day of rejoicing in God, the Father, Almighty, through Jesus Christ of Nazareth, God's only begotten Son, with His Holy Spirit dwelling in us (Zech. 8:19). This is all done, by accepting the atonement Jesus Christ of Nazareth made for us at Passover in 31 A.D., for the forgiveness of our sins. It is by Jesus Christ of Nazareth's stripes that we are healed (Isa. 53:5). Believe on Jesus Christ of Nazareth and let your light shine in Christ Jesus of Nazareth's Holy name. Alleluia and praise the LORD. Amen and Amen.

Continuing the prophecy of Isaiah in the Day of Atonement and the requirement to "…afflict…" our souls, that is, fasting (Lev. 23:27). Isaiah 58:3 says, "Wherefore have we fasted, *say they,* and thou seest not? *wherefore* have we afflicted our soul, and thou takest no knowledge? Behold in the day of your fast ye find pleasure, and exact all your labours.". Jesus had a similar discussion about fasting with John the Baptist's disciples; Jesus compared His own disciples which did not fast, with John's disciples that fasted, and Jesus said, "…Can the children of the bridechamber mourn, as long as the bridegroom is with them? …" (Matt. 9:15). Isaiah 58:4-7 continues, "Behold, ye fast for strife and debate, and to smite with the fist of wickedness: ye shall not fast as *ye* do *this* day, to make your voice to be heard on high. Is it such a fast that I have chosen? a day for a man to afflict his soul? *is it* to bow down his head as a bulrush, and to spread sackcloth and ashes *under him?* Wilt thou call this a fast, and an acceptable day to the LORD? *Is* not this the fast that I have chosen? to loose the bands of wickedness, to undo the heavy burdens, and to let the oppressed go free, and that ye break every yoke? *Is it* not to deal thy bread to the hungry, and that thou bring the poor that are cast out to thy house? When thou seest the naked, that thou cover him; and that thou hide not thyself from thine own flesh?". All of these questions were answered in Jesus Christ of Nazareth. He said of Himself, "Take my yoke upon you…my yoke *is* easy, and my burden is light." (Matt. 11:29, 30). He fed the hungry with bread miraculously multiplied, as well as giving His own flesh on the cross, as the bread from heaven for our eternal salvation (Matt. 14:15-21, 15:32-38; John 6:32-35). He spoke of giving to the poor and covering up the naked; but more importantly, He came to cover up our spiritual nakedness, which is part and parcel to the reason for the writing of this book, as well as my other writings (Matt. 19:21, 25:34-40). Jesus desires us to know the truth, and how the scriptures reveal Himself as the Messiah and our God, the Saviour of this world, and Redeemer of all of mankind. Alleluia and praise the LORD. The point in all of this is, not to suggest fasting is not a good thing, but to understand that God indeed is more focused on the spiritual "doings" of the law rather than the physical afflicting of one's self, first and foremost (John 6:63). It could be suggested the Day of Atonement will literally mark the beginning of the "Messianic age", when and if it comes. As mentioned above, Zechariah says, "Thus saith the LORD of hosts; The fast of the fourth *month,* and the fast of the fifth, and the **fast of the seventh**, and the fast of the tenth, shall be to the house of Judah **joy and gladness**, and **cheerful feast**s; therefore love the truth and peace." (Zech. 8:19). This can take place today, as we serve the living and resurrected Jesus Christ of Nazareth, with God, the Father, through His Holy Spirit. But it may also have a greater fulfillment for this whole world, when or if the "Messianic Age" comes to pass. Alleluia and praise the LORD. Amen and Amen.

Offerings and Sacrifices

As far as offerings and sacrifices go, there are at least two ways of looking at them, the physical offerings and sacrifices, and the spiritual offerings and sacrifices. That being said, the two forms of offerings and sacrifices are not completely unrelated, as I have spoken about in some of my other writings briefly. Nevertheless, let us look at some verses in the Holy Bible of God referring to the different types of offerings and sacrifices that are pleasing to God. Psalm 119:108 says, "Accept, I beseech thee, the freewill offerings of my mouth, O LORD, and teach me thy judgements.". This speaks of our words being a freewill offering. Psalm 50:23 says, "Whoso offereth praise glorifieth me: and to him that ordereth *his* conversation *aright* will I shew the salvation of God.". This would be agreeable with Jesus Christ of Nazareth speaking to His disciples and admonishing us to worship

God in spirit and in truth (John 4:23). Psalm 27:6 says, "And now shall mine head be lifted up above mine enemies round about me: therefore will I offer in his tabernacle sacrifices of joy; I will sing, yea, I will sing praises unto the LORD.". Psalm 4:5 says, "Offer sacrifices of righteousness, and put your trust in the LORD.". These two previous verses are agreeable with the others before them, and prove that God desires us to be righteous and worship Him first and foremost, as an offering pleasing to Him. Alleluia and praise the LORD. Psalm 69:30 and 31 say, "I will praise the name of God with a song, and will magnify him with thanksgiving. *This* also shall please the LORD better than an ox or bullock that hath horns and hoofs.". This is more confirmation of the importance of worshipping God first and foremost; with our own body, mind and soul, before we consider giving Him something outside of ourselves, that is physical. As the scriptures say in the Old Testament, "...thou shalt love the LORD thy God with all thy heart, and with all thy soul, and with all thy might."; and Jesus confirms in the New Testament, "...Thou shalt love the Lord thy God with all thy heart, and with all thy soul, and with all thy mind." (Deut. 6:5, Matt. 22:37, Mark 12:30). Alleluia and praise the LORD. And we must remember that ultimately, it is Jesus Christ of Nazareth, whom gave His life for us on the cross, forgiving us of all of our sins. And He died on that cross at Passover in 31 A.D., spilling His Holy and righteous blood. He was buried and the third day He arose to give us the hope and promise of eternal life in His holy name. Alleluia and praise the LORD. Amen and Amen.

Psalm 40:6 says, "Sacrifice and offering thou didst not desire; mine ears hast thou opened: burnt offering and sin offering hast thou not required.". This was very much fulfilled in Jesus Christ of Nazareth, as He healed the deaf (Matt. 11:4, 5; Mark 7:32-37). But it is also an example for us to open our ears and listen for that still small voice of God speaking to us, through His Holy Spirit in our mind, as we receive Jesus Christ of Nazareth as our Lord and Saviour (1 Kings 19:12). Psalm 50:8-15 says, "I will not reprove thee for thy sacrifices or thy burnt offerings, *to have been* continually before me. I will take no bullock out of thy house, *nor* he goats out of thy folds. For every beast of the forest *is* mine, *and* the cattle upon a thousand hills. I know all the fowls of the mountains: and the wild beasts of the field *are* mine. If I were hungry, I would not tell thee: for the world *is* mine, and the fullness thereof. Will I eat the flesh of bulls, or drink the blood of goats? Offer unto God thanksgiving; and pay thy vows unto the most High: And call upon me in the day of trouble: I will deliver thee, and thou shalt glorify me.". Psalm 51:16-19 says, "For thou desirest not sacrifice; else would I give *it:* thou delightest not in burnt offering. The sacrifices of God *are* a broken spirit: a broken and a contrite heart, O God, thou wilt not despise. Do good in thy good pleasure unto Zion: build thou the walls of Jerusalem. Then shalt thou be pleased with the sacrifices of righteousness, with burnt offering and whole burnt offering: then shall they offer bullocks upon thine altar.". Psalm 66:13-15 says, "I will go into thy house with burnt offerings: I will pay thee my vows, Which my lips have uttered, and my mouth hath spoken, when I was in trouble. I will offer unto thee burnt sacrifices of fatlings, with the incense of rams; I will offer bullocks with goats. Selah.". Strictly speaking, from the perspective of physical offerings in the "Messianic Age" temple, there is listed in Ezekiel's vision, various offerings as follows; burnt offering, sin offering, trespass offering, meat offering, peace offering, and drink offering (Ezek. 40:38, 39; 42:13, 43:27, 45:17). The details of how these offerings are prepared can be found in various places in the Old Testament, much of it, in chapters one to seven of the book of Leviticus. See appendix E for more details on the "Messianic Age". Alleluia and praise the LORD. Amen and Amen.

Conclusion

Jesus' so called "2nd coming"; I have written on this subject in other books I have written, and as the years go on, the way I understand His second coming seems to be changing, as I read more about what Jesus said about it. This idea ties into this chapter and the next well, because of the prophetic example that the Holy days tell about the path we are all headed on here on earth. Jesus said, "…seek ye first the kingdom of God, and his righteousness; and all these things shall be added unto you." (Matt. 6:33). What does this have to do with Jesus' 2nd coming you might ask? It has everything to do with it, Jesus is of God's kingdom, and He said "…the kingdom of God *is* within you." (Luke 9:34, 17:21). He also described the kingdom of God as leaven or a mustard seed, that grows until the whole loaf is leavened, or until the mustard seed has grown into a great tree for birds to hide in (Luke 13:18-21). The point of all of this is, that seeking God's kingdom and experiencing Jesus' 2nd coming, starts with you and I. Trusting and putting our faith in God, the Father, Almighty and Jesus Christ of Nazareth, God's only begotten Son, to fulfil the promises He has made to us, as His children. Jesus said He would be coming in the clouds, and He also said that His coming would be like lightening (Luke 17:24, 21:27). Does this not describe a natural lightning storm perfectly? This is why we need to place our trust in Jesus Christ of Nazareth and the promise that He has sent us His Holy Spirit, marked by the outpouring of the Holy Spirit at Pentecost 31 A.D., as I had described briefly in the previous chapter. Jesus also had authority over storms, which was seen when He rebuked the storm on the lake (Luke 8:24). As well, storms often happen at night, and Jesus is compared to coming as a thief in the night (1 Thess. 5:2, 2 Pet. 3:10, Rev. 3:3, 16:15). The point of all of this, is to help the reader understand that Jesus' 2nd coming is more a process of time, then any specific event necessarily. Albeit, a "Messianic Age", or a 1000 year reign of Christ with His saints, is likely still to come literally, whether they be present physically or spiritually, or both, as of the date of writing this book in 2019 A.D. (Rev. 20:4, 6). The reality is, that when we have the Holy Spirit with us and in us, as believers whom have accepted Jesus Christ of Nazareth as our Saviour; the Kingdom of God dwells IN US, and JESUS dwells in us, and God, the Father, dwell in US! This is the gift of the Holy Spirit, the Comforter, whom will never leave us (John 14:16-18). And Jesus made a promise to all of His disciples, including you and I, saying, "…I am with you alway, *even* unto the end of the world. Amen." (Matt. 28:20). Alleluia and praise the LORD. Amen and Amen.

Isaiah 58:9-14 says, "Then shalt thou call, and the LORD shall answer; thou shalt cry, and he shall say, Here I *am*. If thou take away from the midst of thee the yoke, the putting forth of the finger, and speaking vanity; And *if* thou draw out thy soul to the hungry, and satisfy the afflicted soul; then shall thy light rise in obscurity, and thy darkness *be* as the noon day: And the LORD shall guide thee continually, and satisfy thy soul in drought, and make fat thy bones: and thou shalt be like a watered garden, and like a spring of water, whose waters fail not. And *they that shall be* of thee shall build the old waste places: thou shalt raise up the foundations of many generations; and thou shalt be called, The repairer of the breach, The restorer of paths to dwell in. If thou turn away thy foot from the sabbath, *from* doing thy pleasure on my holy day; and call the sabbath a delight, the holy of the LORD, honourable; and shalt honour him, not doing thine own ways, nor finding thine own pleasure, nor speaking *thine own* words: Then shalt thou delight thyself in the LORD; and I will cause thee to ride upon the high places of the earth, and feed thee with the heritage of Jacob thy father: for the mouth of the LORD hath spoken *it*.". In the next chapter I will continue with the topic of the Holy days, finishing with the feast of Tabernacles and the "Last Great Day". These feast days have, just like the others, historical, present and prophetic significance. Keep reading to learn more. Alleluia and praise the LORD. Amen and Amen.

Discussion: Salvation in Christ Jesus of Nazareth

"...do not sound a trumpet before thee..."
- Matthew 6:2

The book of Joel goes into greater detail about the "great tribulation", and speaks about Jehoshaphat and the valley of decision. The reality is, we all have decisions to make in this life, whether they are simple daily ones, or potentially life changing ones. Jehoshaphat was a king of Judah, and he followed the Lord (1 Kings 22:42-44). One time, the people of Moab and Ammon, descendants of Lot, and people of mount Seir, came to battle Jehoshaphat and the people of the cities of Judah (2 Chr. 20:1). So Jehoshaphat proclaimed a fast and consulted with God about what to do (2 Chr. 20:3-13). Through Jahaziel, a Levite, of the children of Asaph, God said go up to the battle, but the battle would be God's to fight (2 Chr. 20:14-17). Jehoshaphat and his people went up to the battle and stood ready, and they simply praised God (2 Chr. 20:18-22). Miraculously the Moabites and the Ammonites turned on the army of mount Seir and destroyed them, and then turned on one another, and destroyed one another (2 Chr. 20:23). This is the simple and yet truly effective way of "winning" our battles here on earth, first and foremost, in the spiritual realm. That is, we ought to worship the true God only, and serve Him only, first and foremost, and then He will take care of the rest. Jesus said, "But the hour cometh, and now is, when the true worshippers shall worship the Father in spirit and in truth: for the Father seeketh such to worship him.". (John 4:23). We must continually remember that Jesus Christ of Nazareth is the way, the truth and the life (John 14:6). And there is no other name under heaven whereby we can be saved (Acts 4:12). That is, Jesus Christ of Nazareth came for us, while we were yet sinners. He was conceived by the Holy Spirit in and born of the virgin, Mary, espoused to Joseph (Matt. 1:18-25). He was raised a child of Israel, of the tribe of Judah, of the house of David, with brothers and sisters (Matt. 13:55, 56; Luke 2:41-52, Rev. 5:5). He healed, He taught us about all things, and did other miracles, and promised us that He would always be with us through His Holy Spirit (Matt. 28:20, Mark 13:23, John 14:16-18, 26). Alleluia and praise the LORD. Amen and Amen. And most importantly, He spilt His righteous and holy blood on the cross for the forgiveness of our sins and died on the cross at Passover in 31 A.D.. He was buried and the third day He arose, giving us the hope and promise of eternal life in His Holy name. Alleluia and praise the LORD. Amen and Amen.

Discussion Questions

1. What is knowledge, wisdom and understanding?

_____

_____

_____

2.   How do we come to learn the deeper things of God?

_____

_____

_____

CHAPTER 6

Feast of Tabernacles and the Last Great Day

"For the law having a shadow of good things to come..."
- Hebrews 10:1

Introduction

History, Jesus and us, the "Messianic age", the final judgment and the "...new heaven and a new earth...", with the "...new Jerusalem..." (Rev. 20:4, 6, 11-15; 21:1, 2). This previous sentence sums up this world and all whom are in it, from the beginning until a new beginning. See appendix G for a summation of God's 7000 year plan for this present world, that has been spoken about briefly throughout this book. The remainder of this chapter will speak about the final Holy day week of the annual Holy day calendar, the feast of Tabernacles, ending with the last day, on the eighth day of the feast (Lev. 23:33-36, 39-43). These days will be looked at from; a Biblically historical perspective in the Old Testament, their relationship with Jesus Christ of Nazareth, their relevance today, and as a shadow of the good things to come. Read on to learn more. Alleluia and praise the LORD. Amen and Amen.

Feast of Tabernacles

Leviticus 23:34-36 says, "Speak unto the children of Israel, saying, The fifteenth day of this seventh month *shall be* the feast of tabernacles for seven days unto the LORD. On the first day shall be an holy convocation: ye shall do no servile work *therein*. Seven days ye shall offer an offering made by fire unto the LORD: on the eighth day shall be an holy convocation unto you; and ye shall offer an offering made by fire unto the LORD: it *is* a solemn assembly; *and* ye shall do no servile work *therein*.". Leviticus 23:39-43 says, "Also in the fifteenth day of the seventh month, when ye have gathered in the fruit of the land, ye shall keep a feast unto the LORD seven days: on the first day shall be a sabbath, and on the eighth day shall be a sabbath. And ye shall take you on the first day the boughs of goodly trees, branches of palm trees, and the boughs of thick trees, and willows of the brook; and ye shall rejoice before the LORD your God seven days. And ye shall keep it a feast unto the LORD seven days in the year. It shall be a statute for ever in your generations: ye shall celebrate it in the seventh month. That your generations may know that I made the children of Israel to dwell in booths, when I brought them out of the land of Egypt: I am the LORD your God.". Alleluia and praise the LORD. Amen and Amen.

About two weeks after Jesus' birth in 4 B.C., would have been the feast of Tabernacles (Lev. 23:24, 34). Because of Mary, Joseph and Jesus' precarious living circumstances at Jesus' birth, the meaning of the feast of Tabernacles, would likely have been very relevant in their lives at that time, as a time of dwelling in temporary housing (Luke 2:7). At that time of year in 2 B.C., when Jesus was about two years old; Jesus and His parents may have very likely gone into the wilderness of Egypt, fleeing from King Herod, after his proclamation to kill all of the children two years old and under in the area of Jesus' birth (Matt. 2:13-18). I would also suggest Jesus was baptized, at age 30 in 27 A.D., by John, His cousin, John the Baptist, on the first day of the feast of Tabernacles (Matt. 3). After being baptized, He was driven into the wilderness, fasting forty days and forty nights, and then He was tempted by the devil (Matt. 4:1-11). That means, Jesus would have been in the wilderness during the entire feast of Tabernacles in 27 A.D., as He was in the wilderness for forty days (Matt. 4:1-11). This would also represent the temptations and trials the Israelites faced during their forty year wilderness journey, in around 1500 B.C.; as the Bible uses the example of a day for a year in some prophetic interpretations (Ex. 16:35, Num. 14:33, 34; Ezek. 4:6). Jesus partook in the feast of Tabernacles during His earthly ministry, along with His brethren, in Jerusalem; He was discrete at first, letting His brethren go up to Jerusalem before Him, and then He also went and preached in the Temple in the midst of the feast of Tabernacles (John 7:1-24). During that same week, there was revelation by some that Jesus is the Christ, Messiah (John 7:25-44). Jesus' life, in general, was a "cukkah", tabernacle amongst us, Strong's number 5521; "sukkot" is the common plural English spelling of the Hebrew word for booths, tents, etc., Strong's number 5523 (Lev. 23:34, 42). Jesus said, "...the Son of man hath not where to lay *his* head." (Matt. 8:20). This is relevant to all of mankind, as well; as we are given these earthly bodies or "tabernacles", for our spirit and soul to dwell in for a time, and then comes death, our resurrection, and our judgement, and for the faithful, the "...new heaven and a new earth..." with the "...new Jerusalem..." (2 Cor. 5:1, 4; 2 Pet. 1:13, 14; Rev. 21:1, 2). Alleluia and praise the LORD. Amen and Amen.

Jesus and the "Messianic Age"; Luke 14:28-30 says, "For which of you, intending to build a tower, sitteth not down first, and counteth the cost, whether he have *sufficient* to finish *it?* Lest haply, after he hath laid the foundation, and is not able to finish *it,* all that behold *it* begin to mock him, Saying, This man began to build, and was not able to finish.". Ezekiel 40-48 references the workings of the temple in the "Messianic Age", that I have also written about in my other books, namely, "The Daystar and Us". Revelation 20:4 says, "And I saw thrones, and they sat upon them, and judgement was given unto them: and I *saw* the souls of them that were beheaded for the witness of Jesus, and for the word of God, and which had not worshipped the beast, neither his image, neither had received *his* mark upon their foreheads, or in their hands; and they lived and reigned with Christ a thousand years.". Revelation 20:6 says, "Blessed and holy *is* he that hath part in the first resurrection: on such the second death hath no power, but they shall be priests of God and of Christ, and shall reign with him a thousand years.". Zechariah 14:16-19 says, "And it shall come to pass, *that* every one that is left of all the nations which came against Jerusalem shall even go up from year to year to worship the King, the LORD of hosts, and to keep the feast of tabernacles. And it shall be, *that* whoso will not come up of *all* the families of the earth unto Jerusalem to worship the King, the LORD of hosts, even upon them shall be no rain. And if the family of Egypt go not up, and come not, that *have* no *rain;* there shall be the plague, wherewith the LORD will smite the heathen that come not up to keep the feast of tabernacles. This shall be the punishment of Egypt, and the punishment of all nations that come not up to keep the feast of tabernacles.". I have suggested in the book, "The Daystar and Us", that it would be a delegate family from each nation, that would come to celebrate the feast of tabernacles in Jerusalem, each year. See appendix E for more information on the feast of tabernacles and the "Messianic Age". Alleluia and praise the LORD. Amen and Amen.

Last Great Day

Leviticus 23:36 says, "...on the eighth day shall be an holy convocation unto you; and ye shall offer an offering made by fire unto the LORD: it *is* a solemn assembly; *and* ye shall do no servile work *therein*.". Leviticus 23:39 says, "...on the eighth day shall be a sabbath.". This is the eighth day of the feast of tabernacles (Lev. 23:34-36, 39-43). This day marks the end of the Leviticus 23 feasts for the Hebrew calendar year (Ex. 23:16, Lev. 23:44). Alleluia and praise the LORD. Amen and Amen.

Jesus spoke of the "...last day..."; He made a last day resurrection promise (John 6:39, 40, 44, 54). Jesus taught on the "...last day, that great..." day of the feast of tabernacles (John 7:37). Jesus said of Himself, "...If any man thirst, let him come unto me, and drink. He that believeth on me, as the scripture hath said, out of his belly shall flow rivers of living water. (But this spake he of the Spirit, which they that believe on him should receive: for the Holy Ghost was not yet *given;* because that Jesus was not yet glorified.)" (John 7:37-39). The timing of His teaching of this subject on the "...last day..." of the feast of tabernacles is a sign of our need for Jesus Christ of Nazareth for salvation. When that final day arrives, after our death, when we are resurrected and stand before Jesus Christ of Nazareth; it is by His grace and mercy that we are saved from our sinful past, and given a new life; body, soul and spirit, through Jesus Christ of Nazareth's forgiveness of our sins, unto eternal life in His Holy name. This is a free gift from God for those whom believe (Matt. 10:8). It is by faith we are saved, not by our works (Eph. 2:8, 9). Alleluia and praise the LORD. Amen and Amen.

Even Jesus' disciples, namely Martha, knew of the time of the "...last day...", the final resurrection of all of mankind (John 11:23-27). John 11:23-27 says, "Jesus saith unto her, Thy brother shall rise again. Martha saith unto him, I know that he shall rise again in the resurrection at the last day. Jesus said unto her, I am the resurrection, and the life: he that believeth in me, though he were dead, yet shall he live: And whosoever liveth and believeth in me shall never die. Believest thou this? She saith unto him, Yea, Lord: I believe that thou art the Christ, the Son of God, which should come into the world.". This is because they were keeping God's commandments in the first century A.D., in Jerusalem, and in the surrounding land, and as mentioned in this book and in the Holy Bible, God's commanded feast days are a shadow of good things to come (Heb. 10:1). Alleluia and praise the LORD. Amen and Amen.

John 12:44-50 simplifies the judgements and decisions of receiving eternal life in Jesus Christ of Nazareth. It says, "Jesus cried and said, He that believeth on me, believeth not on me, but on him that sent me. And he that seeth me seeth him that sent me. **I am come a light into the world**, that whosoever believeth on me should not abide in darkness. And **if any man hear my words, and believe not, I judge him not: for I came not to judge the world,** but to save the world. He that rejecteth me, and receiveth not my words, hath one that judgeth him: **the word that I have spoken, the same shall judge him in the last day.** For I have not spoken of myself; but **the Father** which sent me, **he gave me a commandment**, what I should say, and what I should speak. And **I know that his commandment is life everlasting**: whatsoever I speak therefore, even as the Father said unto me, so I speak." (John 12:44-50). It should also be noted that this day in the Old Testament commandments is a rest day, and a holy day (Lev. 23:36, 39). We should then consider that the resurrection day, the judgement day of our souls, ought not to be a fearful time or a time to be anxious about. Jesus made it pretty clear, if we believe in Him, we will never die (John 11:26). See appendix C for more on the meaning of the "Last Great Day". Alleluia and praise the LORD. Amen and Amen.

Shadow

After the fall feast days during that time of year, as a new born, after the time of Jesus and His mother's purification was finished, this would be about thirty three days after His birth, about 4 Bul/Heshvan, the eighth month of the Hebrew calendar, or October 25th in 4 B.C. (Lev. 12:4, Luke 2:22-24). He was prophesied over by both a man and a woman at the temple, at this time (Luke 2:25-38). Isaiah 58:2 says, "Yet they seek me daily, and delight to know my ways, as a nation that did righteousness, and forsook not the ordinances of their God; they ask of me the ordinances of justice; they take delight in approaching to God.". The man, Simeon, and the woman, Anna, a widow, no doubt fulfilled this prophecy in the description of Simeon's desire to see the consolation of Israel and Anna, whom served God in the temple day and night; they both prophesied over Jesus at the temple during Jesus' dedication, and Simeon even prophesied over Mary (Luke 2:25-38). As for Jesus and His parents, two years later during the late fall of 2 B.C., after being visited by the "… wise men…", and Joseph being warned in a dream by an angel of the LORD; they likely would have already been enroute if not in Egypt by this time of year, after the fall feast days (Matt. 2:13-15). See appendix B – God's Holydays vs. traditional western Holidays for more information about this. If Jesus was baptized on the first day of the feast of Tabernacles, in 27 A.D., at about the age of thirty, that would be October 4th or 15 Ethanim/Tishri on the Hebrew calendar (Lev. 23:34, Luke 3:21-23). This is the seventh month according to the Biblical reference, called Ethanim, also referenced as Tishri in other references (1 Kings 8:2). That would bring Jesus' time of fasting and temptation in the wilderness to about November 12th or 24 Bul/Heshvan, the eighth month of the Hebrew calendar, in 27 A.D. (1 Kings 6:37). If Jesus' official ministry started about November 13th of 27 A.D., this would make sense, for Jesus' three and a half year earthly ministry, using the day for a year principal to understand Daniel's prophecy of Jesus Christ of Nazareth, as Messiah (Num. 14:34, Ezek. 4:6, Dan. 9:27).Whether you believe Jesus' ministry started at His baptism, during His time of temptation in the wilderness or after He came out of the wilderness in late 27 A.D.; Jesus' ministry, no doubt, likely indeed started in the fall of 27 A.D.. He ministered for three and a half years, healing, forgiving, and doing other miracles. He was then crucified at Passover in 31 A.D., for the forgiveness of our sins, and He died on the cross, spilling His Holy and righteous blood for us. He was buried and the third day He arose to give us the hope and promise of eternal life in His Holy name. Alleluia and praise the LORD. Amen and Amen.

Conclusion

Rejoice in the Lord always (Phil. 4:4). Speaking again of the Kingdom of God, Jesus said, "The law and the prophets *were* until John [John the Baptist], since that time the kingdom of God is preached..." (Luke 16:16). So speaking of the kingdom of God is, according to Jesus Christ of Nazareth, what ought to be preached. I spoke about the idea in the last chapter's conclusion briefly, what the kingdom of God is. And Jesus said, "...Suffer little children...of such is the kingdom of God." (Luke 18:16, 17). I speak of this idea of the kingdom of God, because it is central to having a relationship with God, and enjoying an abundant life here on earth, as well as everlasting life in the name of Jesus Christ of Nazareth (Matt. 6:33, John 10:10). Jesus goes into great detail about the kingdom of God, in the New Testament, and I suggest you consider His words and the Bible; in general, for your greatest knowledge of the kingdom of God. But the kingdom of God, is whom you ought to serve, is whom you ought to follow, and whom you ought to desire to become like. Jesus Christ of Nazareth is essentially, the earthly manifestation of the kingdom of God. If you desire worldly things, they are exactly that, worldly, and your fruits will be of the world, which are in the end coming to not (1 Cor. 7:31). However, if you seek after Jesus Christ of Nazareth and the kingdom of God; you are placing your trust in an immoveable kingdom, and an everlasting kingdom (2 Pet. 1:11). The fruit that you produce of the kingdom of God, in Christ Jesus of Nazareth's Holy name, will outlast any fruit that is born by this world and the lusts thereof. God is a giving, loving and caring God. He is an abundant God, with a storehouse that does not empty, nor does it close (Isa. 9:7, Rev. 21:25). Do not be fooled by the things, experiences, etc., that this world may offer you, for a moment of pleasure or temptation. As the Bible says, "...Resist the devil, and he will flee from you." (Jam. 4:7). I say all of this because God loves you, and Jesus Christ of Nazareth loves you (1 John 4:10). Alleluia and praise the LORD. Amen and Amen.

Jesus Christ of Nazareth laid down His life for you and I. He took all of our sins upon Himself on the cross at Passover in 31 A.D., and has given us everlasting life in return. What greater gift can anybody offer us? There is no greater gift than eternal life in Jesus Christ of Nazareth's Holy name. If you are truly seeking God's kingdom, His truth and true hope; repent, admit you are a sinner and ask Jesus Christ of Nazareth for forgiveness of your sins. Turn to Him and submit your life to Him, you will not regret that you did. This is true freedom and life, that we live a life in the name above all names; the Giver of life, and Creator of this world and all things, the Word become flesh, whom dwelt amongst us, Immanuel, Jesus Christ Immanuel of Nazareth (Acts 4:12). Jesus was conceived by the Holy Spirit in, and born of the virgin, Mary, espoused to Joseph (Matt. 1:18-25). He was raised a child of Israel, of the tribe of Judah, with brothers and sisters (Matt. 13:55, 56; Luke 2:41-52, Rev. 5:5). He taught, healed, forgave and did other miracles for three and a half years, during His earthly ministry. And at Passover in 31 A.D., He was crucified and died on the cross for the forgiveness of our sins, shedding His Holy and righteous blood on the cross. He was buried and the third day He arose to give us the hope and promise of eternal life in His Holy name. Hallelujah and praise the Lord God, the Father, Almighty, and His only begotten Son, Jesus Christ of Nazareth, with His Holy Spirit. The next chapter will speak about the summaries of these previous six chapters, and the final conclusion for this book, in general. Read on to learn more. Alleluia and praise the LORD. Amen and Amen.

Discussion: The Grace of God

"For by grace are ye saved through faith; and that not of yourselves: *it
is* the gift of God: Not of works, lest any man should boast."
- Ephesians 2:8, 9

God, through Moses, speaks in Deuteronomy 9 of Israel possessing the "promised land" of Canaan, after coming out of the wilderness. He says that the people of the land are great and tall, greater and mightier than the Israelites and the Israelites will possess their land (Deut. 9:1, 2). God says He will go before them as a consuming fire and destroy these nations and drive them out before the Israelites face (Deut. 9:3). Deuteronomy 9:4 and 5 say, "Speak not thou in thine heart, after that the LORD thy God hath cast them out from before thee, saying, For my righteousness the LORD hath brought me in to possess this land: but for the wickedness of these nations the LORD doth drive them out from before thee. Not for thy righteousness, or for the uprightness of thine heart, does thou go to possess their land: but for the wickedness of these nations the LORD thy God doth drive them out from before thee, and that he may perform the word which the LORD sware unto thy fathers, Abraham, Isaac, and Jacob.". In the proceeding versus Moses goes on to bring up the things Israel had done in the wilderness to provoke God to anger, and calls Israel a stiffnecked people (Deut. 9:6-26). The point is, that this verse of the Old Testament and part of the books of the law of God, are prophetic in nature, and speak of God's grace towards His called and chosen people. Jesus said of Himself, in the New Testament, "Think not that I am come to destroy the law, or the prophets: I am not come to destroy, but to fulfil." (Matt. 5:17). The apostle, Paul, speaks of the "...law of Christ..." (Gal. 6:2). The point is, that Jesus Christ of Nazareth is "...I AM...", and God does not change (Ex. 3:14, Isa. 43:13, Mal. 3:6, John 8:58). God, the Father, with His only begotten Son, Jesus Christ of Nazareth, the Word become flesh, and the Holy Ghost, were with the Israelites in the wilderness, they were with Abraham before that, and they were in the beginning before the day light was created (Gen. 1:2, Isa. 43:13, John 1:1, 14; 1 Cor. 10:4). So if there is to come a prophetic "Messianic Age", and the feast of tabernacles is a prophetic sign of the "Messianic Age" to come, as of the date of writing this book in 2019 A.D.; we need not be worried or concerned about our part in "making" it come to pass. It is God, the Father, Almighty, whom does the work in us and through us and around us through His Holy Spirit, the Holy Ghost; it is in Jesus Christ of Nazareth's Holy name we are saved, "Messianic Age" or no "Messianic Age". And the Holy Bible says of Jesus, "And when he was demanded of the Pharisees, when the kingdom of God should come, he answered them and said, The kingdom of God cometh not with observation: Neither shall they say, Lo here! or, lo there! for, behold, the kingdom of God is within you." (Luke 17:20, 21). Alleluia and praise the LORD. Amen and Amen. Read on to open your mind to whatever God wills you, regarding your relationship with Him today, the possibilities in the "Messianic Age", and forever more in the "world to come". Alleluia and praise the LORD. Amen and Amen.

Discussion Questions

1. God speaks of the power of our tongue; what changes can you make in your communication, to speak life into this world and others?

_____

_____

_____

2. In the "Messianic age", the Levites are restored to their position of authority in teaching the commands of God to the people. How might this change from today's world?

_____

_____

_____

CHAPTER 7

Summaries and Conclusion

"For God so loved the world, that he gave his only begotten Son, that whosoever believeth in him should not perish, but have everlasting life."
- John 3:16

Chapter One Summary

Chapter one spoke about the creation of the sun and the moon; and there purposes for signs, and for the keeping of time. The two time keeping methods of this world were spoken of; that is the solar calendar system, and the lunar calendar system. And it was determined that these two systems are not necessarily unrelated to one another. As Genesis 1:14 and 15 say, "And God said, Let there be lights in the firmament of the heaven to divide the day from the night: and let them be for signs, and for seasons, and for days, and years: And let them be for lights in the firmament of the heaven to give light upon the earth: and it was so.". Alleluia and praise the LORD. Amen and Amen.

Chapter Two Summary

Chapter two went into greater detail about time keeping, namely, it spoke about the seventh day, sabbath day of rest, that was instituted on the seventh day of creation, as God ended His work and rested on the seventh day, and sanctified that day (Gen. 2:1-3). And there was some discussion about Jesus Christ of Nazareth and His crucifixion week, and when the events of that week took place. Namely, Jesus Christ of Nazareth was crucified on a Wednesday, at Passover in 31 A.D., dying on the cross for the forgiveness of our sins. He was buried and He arose the third day, sometime late Saturday, being three days and three nights in the grave, in accordance with the sign of Jonah (Matt. 12:39, 40). Then He revealed Himself to His disciples the first day of the week, Sunday, first to Mary Magdalene near His sepulchre; giving us all the hope and promise of the resurrection and life eternal in Jesus Christ of Nazareth's Holy name (Mark 16:9). There was also some discussion about what day of the week ought to be kept, as the Biblical Sabbath, namely Saturday, the seventh day of the week. Alleluia and praise the LORD. Amen and Amen.

Chapter Three Summary

Chapter three discussed the first feast of the annual Holy days, namely of Passover, and the feast of unleavened bread, along with the offering of the sheaf of the firstfruits, to wave before the LORD, the day after the first Sabbath, after Passover (Lev. 23:5-14). Also discussed, was their purpose in the Old Testament, Jesus Christ of Nazareth's fulfillment in them, their relevance today, and as a sign of good things come (Heb. 10:1). Alleluia and praise the LORD. Jesus said, "...This is the work of God, that ye believe on him whom he hath sent." (John 6:29). I had often thought that this was a strange way of explaining our faith in Christ Jesus of Nazareth; but understanding the offering He made on the cross, puts this command into perfect perspective. We are to believe "on" the works, that Jesus did on the cross at Passover in 31 A.D.. Believe that He died on the cross for the forgiveness of our sins, spilling His Holy and righteous blood on the cross at Passover in 31 A.D.. Believe that He has forgiven us, He was buried and He arose from the dead three days later (Luke 23:34). And believe that Jesus Christ of Nazareth has given us eternal life in His Holy name (John 17:3). It is the works of God ON the cross, by Jesus Christ of Nazareth, that we are forgiven and saved, and this is a free gift. Have you accepted these works of God for the forgiveness of your sins, and salvation in Jesus Christ of Nazareth? He has been resurrected to give us a hope and a promise of eternal life in His Holy name. And He will come into your life and dwell with you, and in you, if you ask Him to (Luke 11:13, John 14:16-18). I promise you this, He loves you! Have you accepted Jesus Christ of Nazareth, as Lord of your life? If so, praise the Lord. Jesus Christ of Nazareth is the Lord of us all. Alleluia and praise the LORD. Amen and Amen.

Chapter Four Summary

Chapter four discussed the feast of harvest or the feast of weeks, also known as Pentecost in the New Testament (Ex. 23:16, 34:22; Lev. 23:15-22). The practical purpose of this feast's origin was discussed, namely in agricultural practices, along with Jesus' fulfilment in them, especially through the outpouring of His Holy Spirit at Pentecost in 31 A.D., onto His disciples, and on all whom believe after that, along with the relevance of the Holy day today, and in what is to come (Acts 2:1-4). Alleluia and praise the LORD. Amen and Amen.

Chapter Five Summary

Chapter five discussed the first two fall Holy days; the feast of Trumpets, and the Day of Atonement (Lev. 23:23-32). These two Holy days were discussed in their historical light of the Old Testament, in the light of Jesus Christ of Nazareth, and His fulfillment in them, namely regarding His birth, likely on the feast of Trumpets in 4 B.C. (Luke 2:8-18). And the chapter also discussed the two fall Holy days' relevance for us today, and in the good things to come. Alleluia and praise the LORD. Amen and Amen.

Chapter Six Summary

Last, in chapter six, we discussed the final Holy week, of the annual feast days, that is, the feast of Tabernacles, culminating with the "...last day..." of the feast, on the eighth day of the feast (Lev. 23:33-36, 39-43; John 6:39). These days are remembered as a sign of the Israelites whom came out of Egypt, and dwelt in the wilderness for forty years before entering the promised land of Canaan, where their ancestors; Abraham, Isaac and Jacob, dwelt in, before them. The feast of Tabernacles was also related to Jesus, and the likelihood that He and His parents fled to Egypt in 2 B.C., at that time of year, when Jesus was a young child of about two years old, in order to escape king Herod, and his desire to destroy the Messiah (Matt. 2:13-15). It was also suggested that Jesus Christ of Nazareth was baptized by John the Baptist, Jesus' cousin, at the beginning of this feast week, in 27 A.D., at about the age of thirty, right before He went into the wilderness to fast for forty days and forty nights, then tempted by the devil (Luke 3:21-23, 4:1-13). Then after this, likely in the eighth month of the Hebrew calendar year, in 27 A.D., He started His miracle working ministry, healing, forgiving sin, and the like, for three and a half years. And at Passover, three and a half years later, in 31 A.D., Jesus Christ of Nazareth, died on the cross for the forgiveness of our sins, shedding His Holy and righteous blood. He was buried and the third day He arose to give us the hope and promise of eternal life in His Holy name. Alleluia and praise the LORD. Amen and Amen.

Conclusion

God's salvation plan for mankind is displayed in His Holydays; that continue throughout the calendar year, each calendar year, forever (Lev. 23, Rev. 14:6). It is those whom have kept the feasts, whom have the knowledge of the "greater plan" God has, for each and every one of us. As the Bible says, they are "...a shadow of good things to come..." (Heb. 10:1). When we are called to dwell in God; are we not being called to be obedient to Him, and to observe His Holy days of feasting and of rest (1 John 2:3; 5:2, 3)? We can also abide in the shadow of the cross of Jesus Christ of Nazareth, and His burial; however, we also have the light, in His life and resurrection, with the promise of our own life and resurrection in Jesus Christ of Nazareth's Holy name. Alleluia and praise the LORD. The good news about Jesus Christ of Nazareth is, that He came not only for the Jews, but also for the lost sheep of the house of Israel; and again, not only did He come for Judah and the lost sheep of the house of Israel, but He came for the Gentiles as well (Matt. 10:6, John 10:16). All of the nations of the world that have been founded since Noah and his sons walked off of the ark with their wives. Is this not an interesting and remarkable truth!? Jesus came to save you and I, regardless of the colour of our skin, what culture or "religion" we come from, regardless of where we were born, or what sins we or our ancestors have committed. Jesus came to save us all! God desires to save all of mankind! Have you accepted the Creator of the universe, the Creator of the heavens and the earth into your life? Have you accepted the "...Lord...of the sabbath day."; Jesus Christ of Nazareth, to wash away your sins (Matt. 12:8)? If you have said yes, great! If not, what are you waiting for? Jesus Christ of Nazareth desires all of us to receive eternal life, this means YOU and I. Say a simple prayer to God, admitting you are a sinner, asking for forgiveness is Jesus Christ of Nazareth's Holy name and invite His Holy Spirit into your life; body, soul and spirit. You will be glad you have. When you do this, you now have the Advocate of the Father with you (1 John 2:1, 2). Alleluia and praise the LORD. The promised Holy Spirit, that Jesus said would be sent to us, after His ascent to God, the Father (John 14:16-18, 16:7-11). It is this Spirit, the Holy Spirit of God, which gives us life in Jesus Christ of Nazareth's Holy name, and will resurrect us again at the last "…great…" day (John 7:37). The scripture says, Jesus "…will never leave thee, nor forsake thee." (Heb. 13:5). He will always be with us, and in us, this means forever! The giver of life has and will give you everlasting life in His Holy name! Just accept His free gift. Alleluia and praise the LORD. Amen and Amen.

I do not desire to discount all of what I have written, but the Bible does say both in the New and Old Testament that "…The just shall live by faith." (Hab. 2:4, Rom. 1:17). The Bible does also say that "…faith without works is dead…" (Jam. 2:20). But I would plead with you, first and foremost, to place your trust in Jesus Christ of Nazareth, for the truth of how to go about your daily life. Regardless of what your situation is, if you think you are being called to observe Holy days, great. There are many organizations in this world, whom keep them in some form or fashion, as of the date of writing this book in 2019 A.D.. But these decisions need to be personal, first and foremost, committing our life to Christ is exactly that. Committing our life to Jesus Christ of Nazareth, not to men, not to the commandments of men (1 Cor. 7:23, Titus 1:14). Keep this in mind, when you are deciding how to move forward with any information you may have learned in this book. A life for Jesus Christ of Nazareth is a life worth living. As the scriptures say, "…ye know that your labour is not in vain in the Lord." (1 Cor. 15:58). There is a promise, both in this life and in "…the world to come…", that Christ has promised us (Mark 10:30). As Jesus says of Himself, "…I go to prepare a place for you. And if I go and prepare a place for you, I will come again, and receive you unto myself; that where I am, *there* ye may be also." (John 14:2, 3). Jesus Christ of Nazareth is eternal, and He has and is preparing an eternal place, in His eternal house, for us to dwell in, with Him, forever (John 14:1-4). As the Bible says, "…the fashion of this world passeth away." (1 Cor. 7:31). And Jesus said of God, the Father, and Himself, "…this is life eternal, that they might know thee the only true God, and Jesus Christ, whom thou hast sent." (John 17:3). It is this same relationship that has us cry, "…Abba, Father." (Rom. 8:15). He loves us, He cares for us, He has died on the cross for us, for the forgiveness of our sins, He was buried and He has risen the third day to give us the hope and promise of eternal life in Jesus Christ of Nazareth's Holy name. It is in Jesus Christ of Nazareth that we have life and He loves us. He loves you forever. Alleluia and praise the LORD. Amen and Amen.

Last, there is life and freedom in Jesus Christ of Nazareth (John 8:32, 14:6). The commandments are great and will guide a person to Jesus Christ of Nazareth, eventually, if followed. But it is only Jesus Christ of Nazareth that truly makes us free (John 8:32, 14:6). He is the fulfilment of the law, after all (Matt. 5:17). The Old Testament mentions the "…sacrifice of praise…"; this is what God desires (Jer. 33:11). How difficult a life is it really in following the Almighty? All He asks of us, is praise, and recognition of His greatness; but not out of selfishness, He desires us to share in His greatness and glory (John 17:22, 23). This is the selfless, loving, graceful, merciful and abundant God that we serve. And His love was shown through the life of His only begotten Son, Jesus Christ of Nazareth; it is spoken of in the Scriptures and continues to be revealed to us through true signs, wonders and miracles. We serve a living God and loving God and an infinitely forgiving God. There is abundance and never ending increase of life in Jesus Christ of Nazareth, the only begotten Son of God, with God, the Father, Almighty, through the indwelling of His Holy

Spirit (John 10:10). He was born a sinless man, the only begotten Son of God, conceived by the Holy Spirit in and born of the virgin, Mary, espoused to Joseph (Matt. 1:18-25). He was raised a child of Israel, of the tribe of Judah, with brothers and sisters (Matt. 13:55, 56; Luke 2:41-52, Rev. 5:5). He began His ministry at about the age of thirty, and for three and a half years, He taught, healed, forgave and did other miracles (Luke 3:23). And at Passover in 31 A.D., He died on the cross for the forgiveness of our sins, shedding His Holy and righteous blood. He was buried and He arose the third day to the glory of God and to give us the hope and resurrection promise of eternal life in Jesus Christ of Nazareth's Holy name. Have you received this gift of eternal life in the name of Jesus Christ of Nazareth? Ask Christ to come into your life; body, soul and mind, accepting the Holy Spirit to cleanse you of your sins, through Jesus' shed blood on the cross, giving you a new life of obedience to God, the Father, Almighty in Jesus Christ of Nazareth's Holy name, through His Holy Spirit. He promises of Himself, "...I am with you alway, *even* unto the end of the world. Amen." (Matt. 28:20). Ask Him in prayer and He will come into you. Praise the Lord God, the Father, Almighty, and His only begotten Son, Jesus Christ of Nazareth, with His Holy Spirit. Alleluia and praise the LORD. Amen and Amen.

Discussion: Peace

"Great peace have they which love thy law: and nothing shall offend them."
- Psalm 119:165

In my later stages of writing my books, as I started writing the third to seventh books congruently, but finishing them separately, various Bible verses came into mind, that had been remembered from previous leisure reading. The idea of the fruits of the Holy Spirit, and Jesus commanding us not to blaspheme the Holy Spirit was paramount in my mind for at least a week (Mark 3:28, 29; Gal. 5:22, 23). The point is, that one of the fruits of the Holy Spirit is peace (Gal. 5:22). And if this is one of the fruits of the Holy Spirit, then we ought not to reject peace, or else we are in danger of hell fire (Mark 3:28, 29). Not only this, but if we have the peace of the Holy Spirit, which passes all understanding, and apply it to Psalm 119:165, nothing shall offend us. This may seem like a tall order in a world that we have little to no control over, but that is why we have Jesus Christ Immanuel of Nazareth. He said that He did not come to condemn, but to save (John 3:17). He calls us to forgive (Matt. 18:21-35). And He calls us to be at peace with all men (Rom. 12:18, Heb. 12:14). The reality is that we cannot work to produce this peace; it is a gift from God, like everything else is (Eph. 2:8, 9). So there is no need to be anxious or impatient about receiving this or any other of the fruits of the Holy Spirit, as they come from God freely, in the name of His only begotten Son, Jesus Christ of Nazareth. He died on the cross for the forgiveness of our sins, shedding His Holy and righteous blood at Passover in 31 A.D.. He was buried and the third day, He arose to give us the hope and promise of eternal life in His Holy name. Alleluia and praise the LORD. Amen and Amen.

Discussion Questions

1. What should we do now that we have this information?

    _____

    _____

    _____

2. Who is the ultimate provider of all things? Find some verses in the Bible that confirm your thinking.

    _____

    _____

    _____

Afterword

How can I or anyone else argue that the "Old Testament" commandments of God are still relevant today? Or how can I or anyone else argue that the "Old Testament" commandments are not relevant today? The apostle, Paul, was one of the best to argue both for and against following the commandments (Rom. 2:12, 13; Eph. 2:15-17). Was Paul doubleminded in his letters? I think not, but he was struggling with his Jewish faith and beliefs in God, in attempting always, unto death to relate with the gentiles and their faith in God, whom did not know the commandments of God, as the Jews did; but only by their own traditions and conscience did they do what they thought was "right" (Rom. 2:14-16). But more than that, Paul, and all of the other New Testament authors were saying that Jesus is the answer to the commandments of God. Jesus is the fulfillment of the law after all (Matt. 5:17)! Jesus said He, Himself, did not come to abolish the law but to fulfil it (Matt. 5:17-19). In a psalm it says, "The LORD preserveth the simple..." (Ps. 116:6). The apostle, Paul, said that in Christ is simplicity (2 Cor. 11:3). Truly, there are three simple steps to salvation in Christ Jesus of Nazareth; repent, that is, turn from evil, believing on the name of Jesus Christ of Nazareth for the forgiveness of your sins; forgive others in Jesus Christ of Nazareth's Holy name; and receive His Holy Spirit, which is a gift given to us freely (Eph. 2:8, 9). If you have done this you are saved (Rom. 10:13). Pray to God, the Father, Almighty, through His Holy Spirit, in the name of Jesus Christ of Nazareth, God's only begotten Son, to help lead you all of the days of your life here on earth and forever more. You will not regret it. Alleluia and praise the LORD. Amen and Amen.

King David said in a psalm, that the "...commandment *is* exceedingly broad." (Ps. 119:96). I have searched and read the Old Testament law and commandments, and although I do not think I could list them all, if someone asked me, I have learned somethings about them. I know that what David is saying is true, about God's command. The law is "...broad...", in that it covers all of life experience. That is, the law and the prophets and the Bible, in general, is relevant to all of us. Whether we are a little child, a teenager, in our 20's, 30's, 40's, 50's, 60's, 70's or 80's and so on. Whether we are sinners or "saintly" so to speak; it is relevant to criminals, family, stay at home moms, business people, and the list will go on. The point is, that the commandments are made in such a way that they help grow us in our relationship with God and others. We can commit sin, but I have found that the Scriptures and the law are actually very merciful and graceful, forgiving, "...exceedingly broad..." in the way we follow them (Ps. 119:96). Of course, there is one Scripture for the "authority" and another for whom must submit to the "authority". But this is where Christ comes in, and this is where the love of God comes in. Jesus Christ of Nazareth said of Himself, "...I am the way, the truth, and the life: no man cometh unto the Father, but by me." (John 14:6). No matter who we are in this life and how we keep God's commands, we all have to meet the same standard someday, and that standard is set in Jesus Christ of Nazareth. As the Bible says, "...there is none other name under heaven given among men, whereby we must be saved." (Acts 4:12). Alleluia and praise the LORD. Amen and Amen.

Last, the apostle, John, spoke candidly in His letters about loving God by keeping God's commandments (1 John 5:1-5, 2 John 1-7). Of course, the greatest commandment is to love God, and obey Him (Deut. 11:13, 14; Matt. 22:37). And Jesus gave a new commandment, to love one another, as Jesus loves us (John 13:34). Believing in and on Jesus Christ of Nazareth, whom came in the flesh, and accepting His Holy Spirit into your life would be the greatest thing you could do in this life (John 1:14, 14:1, 17:20, 21; Gal. 5:22, 23). Admitting you are a sinner and accepting His gift of forgiveness by the blood sacrifice of His life on the cross, is the greatest thing you could do in this life. Jesus was conceived by the Holy Spirit in and born of the virgin, Mary, espoused to Joseph (Matt. 1:18-25). He was raised, a child of Israel, of the tribe of Judah, with brothers and sisters (Matt. 13:55, 56; Luke 2:41-52, Rev. 5:5). He began His ministry at about the age of thirty in the fall of 27 A.D., and taught, healed, forgave and did other miracles for three and a half years (Luke 3:23). And at Passover in 31 A.D., He was crucified and died on the cross for the forgiveness of our sins, shedding His Holy and righteous blood. He was buried and the third day He arose to give us all the hope and promise of eternal life in His Holy name. Alleluia and praise the LORD. What is stopping you from accepting the gift of eternal life in Jesus Christ of Nazareth? No matter the excuse, take that leap of faith and step into a life in Christ Jesus of Nazareth. I promise, you will never be the same, and all for the better. Alleluia and praise the LORD. Amen and Amen.

Appendices

APPENDIX A

Solar vs. Lunar Calendar

Lunar Month	Name(s)	Reference
First Month	Nisan (Abib)	Neh. 2:1, Est. 3:7 (Ex. 13:4, 23:15, 34:18; Deut. 16:1)
Second Month	Zif	1 Kings 6:1
Third Month	Sivan	Est. 9:9
Forth Month	Tammuz	Internet, https://www.chabad.org/library/article_cdo/ aid/2263474/jewish/Tammuz.htm, retrieved 27/04/2022
Fifth Month	Av	Internet, https://www.chabad.org/library/article_cdo/ aid/2263460/jewish/Av.htm, retrieved 27/04/2022
Sixth Month	Elul	Neh. 6:15
Seventh Month	Ethanim	1 Kings 8:2
Eighth Month	Bul	1 Kings 6:38
Ninth Month	Chisleu	Zech. 7:1
Tenth Month	Tebeth	Est. 2:16
Eleventh Month	Sebat	Zech. 1:7
Twelfth Month	Adar	Est. 3:7

*Thirteenth Month – Just like the solar calendar, the Lunar calendar needs to account for approximations, this is done by adding an extra month on the 3rd, 6th, 8th, 11th, 14th, 17th, and 19th year, every nineteen solar years, according to http://www.jewfaq.org/calendar.htm**, retrieved 17/08/2018. The extra month is referred to as Adar I, while the original Adar is called Adar II.**

See http://atlanta.clclutheran.org/bibleclass/hebrewcalendar.html, retrieved Dec. 12, 2016, to see a Hebrew calendar year compared to the Gregorian system in an image. Any month name differences from Biblical references are due to possible translation differences.

APPENDIX B

God's Holydays vs. traditional western Holidays

Introduction

This subject could be written about from various different angles and has been from various religious organizations, including those whom profess to follow Jesus Christ of Nazareth. Before going into too much detail about the similarities and differences between the two types of annual feast seasons, let me speak about the history of the people of Israel in all of this. I will mention this again below, but I believe, and I wrote a book about it, "Origin of Mankind", that the main reason for the differences are because of Israel's rebellion over 2500 years ago, as of the date of writing this book in 2019 A.D.. Israel had rebelled and went into captivity starting in about 700 B.C., bringing their mix of proper worship of God, with idolatry into the places they went into captivity to (1 Kings 12:26-33, 2 Kings 15:29). Centuries earlier, around 1030 B.C., the Danites, a tribe of Israel, had already fallen into idolatry and took a Levite priest for themselves, to worship God in their own way (Jud. 18). This is the history of Israel, and it even started before this, when they were in the wilderness and Moses was upon Mount Sinai, receiving the Ten Commandments from God. They grew tired of waiting for Moses and they provoked Aaron, Moses' older brother, the priest of the people, to build an idolatrous golden calf for them to worship (Ex. 32). This is one of the earliest examples of ancient Israel's rebellion from the true God; even after all of the miracles God did for our ancestors, after taking them out of captivity from the Pharaoh of Egypt (Ex. 7-11). It would seem we never learn, and this is why Jesus Christ of Nazareth is so important to the history of Israel and for mankind, in general. He came humbly as a child, born into a common Israelite family, of the lineage of David, of the tribe of Judah, conceived miraculously by the Holy Spirit in, and born of the virgin, Mary, espoused to Joseph (Matt. 1:18-25, Rev. 5:5). He was raised a child of Israel, with brothers and sisters, the Son of man, but was God's only begotten Son, whom taught of the kingdom of God and repentance for the forgiveness of our sins in His Holy name by the perfect blood offering He gave to us on the cross at Passover in 31 A.D. (Luke 2:41-52). Alleluia and praise the Lord. He died on the cross at Passover in 31 A.D., He was buried and He arose the third day to give us the hope and promise of eternal life in His Holy name. This should be the "main" purpose of the Bible, and any Holyday, Holiday, etc., that we keep. Keep this in mind when reading the remainder of this appendix, this entire book and living life, in general. Praise the LORD God, the Father, Almighty and His only begotten Son, Jesus Christ of Nazareth, with His Holy Spirit. Alleluia and praise the LORD. Amen and Amen.

Passover and Easter

At this time of year some young children may be thinking about Easter chocolate surprises, Easter morning, and parents and older children are thinking about their own responsibilities, as of the date of writing this book in 2019 A.D.. The ground is defrosting, in the North anyhow, and spring is starting to show itself. It is a time we look forward to, in warming up weather, renewal of our own life and preparing for some new growth on the earth. This time of year may have many meanings to many people, but there was one event that took place at Passover in 31 A.D., that would change this world forever. In this section, I will talk about Christ, His sacrifice for the forgiveness of our sins, His burial and His resurrection, three days later, for our hope and promise of eternal life in His Holy name. Alleluia and praise the LORD. First, I will admit this time of year did not mean much to me spiritually during my teens and early 20's. I was just happy that warmer weather was coming along, so I could wear shorts again and spend more time outside in the sun. But now that I am a "little" more grown-up, this time of year has become one of much deeper meaning and a time of reflection. When I was young, I looked forward to chocolate on Easter morning, and I suppose I had a childlike understanding that Christ had died on the cross for the forgiveness of our sins, He was buried and He was resurrected three days later, for us to have eternal life. But beyond that I did not think into it too much. Alleluia and praise the LORD. Amen and Amen.

Since growing older and desiring to learn more about whom Christ actually is, I found out that His crucifixion was simple, but there was more background and meaning to it then I had known as a child. I learned that He was crucified on Passover, which was an Israelite festival, celebrated by slaughtering the Passover lamb, originally for laying the blood on the door posts and lintel of the home, to protect the Israelites, during the "Plague of death" in the Exodus account of the Bible (Ex. 12:23). Not only this, but there were days after the Passover that were instituted that represent removing sin from our life, "The days of unleavened bread", as mentioned in chapter three of this book (Ex. 34:18; Deut. 16:3; 1 Cor. 5:7, 8). This is what makes me think a little more about what Christ did for us and what He is asking us to do for Him and others. Of course, more popularly, at least in the majority of Christianity today, Lent, is spent as a time of reflection and "fasting" of some sort, to remember Christ's forty days in the wilderness when He was fasting (Matt. 4:1-11). But for those whom choose to observe it, this can be a time of more than just fasting; it can be a time of reflection, questioning, prayer, and planning. What direction am I or are you heading in on our life's journey? What do we look forward to over this year ahead? Are you headed on the right course, or do you need to adjust your bearings some? This is our opportunity to question, what do we really desire to do with this wonderful gift of life God has given us? Or a better question yet, what does God desire to do with our life? Alleluia and praise the LORD. Amen and Amen.

Answers for some of the questions we have, may not always be readily available, but if we take time to reflect, talk to others, pray and dig into God's Word, I think you will find that the answers will come (Matt. 7:7, 8). I think most importantly, we should remember that we have a Living, Loving God, who gave His only begotten Son, Jesus Christ of Nazareth, to come down to earth to show us how life is meant to be lived. We serve a God that is alive, that has a plan for us, and that loves us so much that He gave, His only begotten Son, to die on the cross for the forgiveness of our sins. Not only this, but He was buried and He arose the third day to show us that we have the same opportunity as Him. That is, that we have an opportunity to have eternal life, through faith in Christ Jesus of Nazareth (John 3:16). Alleluia and praise the LORD. Are you ready to give your life over to Christ and follow His Eternal plan for you? Is He the Son of God? No doubt. Was He a man on earth? No doubt. Has He been resurrected to conquer death forever? There is no doubt in my mind. He did this all to give us hope, not only to make it through the tough times in this life, but to show us that God's plan for us is much more long term than today or tomorrow. He has an Eternal plan for us. He desires us to live and reign with Him forever. Keep this in mind, when you reflect on your part in this world we live in today. God has a plan for you (Jer. 29:11). He is not and will never give up on fulfilling His promises He has for you and I. Put your faith in Jesus Christ of Nazareth and He will lead you to your "Promised Land". Alleluia and Praise the LORD. Amen and Amen.

The Feast of Tabernacles and Thanksgiving

Pilgrims and strangers in the earth; the children of Israel are considered as such, but those whom do not descend from the children of Israel, are also considered strangers (Lev. 19:34, Heb. 11:13). Nevertheless, if you believe it, we all came from our common ancestors; Japheth, Shem and Ham; Noah being those men's father, in about 2400 B.C., and about 1600 years before them, from Adam and Eve, in the beginning (Gen. 3, 5:32). Our ancestors have sojourned in the wilderness of life; we have been through many toils and trials, waiting for the true God of Israel and the whole world to fulfill His promises to us. Jesus Christ of Nazareth was, is and is to come, the fulfillment of all of God's promises to the children of Israel, the "...lost sheep of the house Israel.", and to the sheep not of this fold, the gentile nations of this world (Matt. 10:6, John 10:16). God loves us all, and He showed this perfectly through the earthly life, death on the cross for the forgiveness of our sins, burial and resurrection after three days, of His only begotten Son, Jesus Christ of Nazareth. Whom died on the cross for the forgiveness of our sins at Passover in 31 A.D., He was buried and He arose the third day to give us the hope and promise of eternal life in His Holy name. Alleluia and Praise the Lord. Prophecy will still be fulfilled as God wills it, and in His timing, but we must wholly put our trust in Him for all of this, in the name of His only begotten Son, Jesus Christ Immanuel of Nazareth. Alleluia and praise the Lord. Amen and Amen.

God spoke to Jacob, and Jacob in turn prophesied over his sons, what would befall them, and us, their descendants in the last days (Gen. 49). There is more prophecy in the Bible of our falling away in the last days (Dan. 10:14, 11:35; 2 Thess. 2:3). Jesus prophesied of it; hatred would grow, people's hearts would wax cold, nation would rise against nation, etc., as of the date of writing this book in 2019 A.D. (Matt. 24). I have written books on the subjects, but the Bible does a perfect job of explaining all of this, by the inspiration of the Holy Spirit in us. The point in all of this is, to explain in simple terms, why the divisions, vexations and all confusions have taken place in this world, that is, because of rebellion against God, and against true worship of Him. As the Psalmist said, "They are all gone aside, they are all together become filthy: there is none that doeth good, no, not one." (Ps. 14:3). Psalm 53:3 says, "Every one of them is gone back: they are altogether become filthy; *there is* none that doeth good, no, not one.". Jesus confirms this, even condemning Himself. Matthew 19:16-21 says, "And, behold, one came and said unto him, Good Master, what good thing shall I do, that I may have eternal life? And he said unto him, Why callest thou me good? *there is* none good but one, *that is,* God: but if thou wilt enter into life, keep the commandments. He saith unto him, Which? Jesus said, Thou shalt do no murder, Thou shalt not commit adultery, Thou shalt not steal, Thou shalt not bear false witness, Honour thy father and *thy* mother: and, Thou shalt love thy neighbour as thyself. The young man saith unto him, All these things have I kept from my youth up: what lack I yet? Jesus said unto him, If thou wilt be perfect, go *and* sell that thou hast, and give to the poor, and thou shalt have treasure in heaven: and come *and* follow me.". This is what Jesus Christ of Nazareth is asking us to do. Alleluia and praise the LORD. Amen and Amen.

Traditionally, in the west at least, a day has been set aside for thanksgiving, it has been attributed to the pilgrims of the 16th century and is no doubt associated with the freedoms and liberties they received in this new land they had come to, in part prophesied by God to be given to the children of Israel, namely the descendants of Ephraim, Manasseh and Naphtali in the west (Gen. 48, 49:21, 22-26; Deut. 33:13-17,

23).[16] This subject is spoken of in greater detail in my book, "Origin of Mankind", and the Bible speaks of these prophecies being fulfilled in detail. This is, no doubt, where the different religious sects, even within Christianity and Judaism have come from, especially in the west today. From the various organizations that continually branch off from one another, because of the disagreement of one doctrine or another, but ultimately this has all had a greater purpose, in order to reveal the truth of God's plan for all of mankind; and, that is, ultimately salvation is in no other name, but that of Jesus Christ of Nazareth. Alleluia and praise the LORD. As the Bible says, "Rejoice in the Lord alway: *and* again I say, Rejoice." (Phil. 4:4). Again as the Bible says, "…all things work together for good to them that love God…" (Rom. 8:28). And we know we love God, by this, that we keep His commandments (John 18:21). And as Jesus Christ of Nazareth said and did, "Greater love hath no man than this, that a man lay down his life for his friends." (John 15:13). This is, in the words of John Newton, the 17th century British sea captain convert to Christ, "Amazing grace, how sweet the sound, that saved a wretch like me.". Praise and worship the true God, the Father, in Jesus Christ of Nazareth's Holy name, God's only begotten Son, with His Holy Spirit. Alleluia and praise the LORD. Amen and Amen.

The Last Great Day and Halloween

I could get into all sorts of ideas of "pagan" and/or occult practices that Halloween may have some sort of traditional roots in. However, I would also like to talk about the other possible roots of Halloween. That are not so much historically proven as far as I know, however these ideas may "enlighten" the way you look at the day in general. I will do this speaking of some of the traditional days that surround this time of year. Certainly, the Bible does talk about sorcery and wickedness as being an abomination to the Lord (Deut. 18:10, 11). So anyone who practices "sorcery" and the worshipping of the dead as a common practice may want to consider why they are practicing such beliefs. It may be from a tradition in upbringing or picked up in some cultural practice as we grew up. An example of this from the Bible may be when King Saul consulted a medium to speak with the dead prophet Samuel. Samuel was none too pleased when he was "awoken" from his slumber (1 Sam. 28:7-29). But the point is; God is a God of the living, not of the dead and we ought to worship and obey the living God, first and foremost (Luke 20:38, Ex. 20:3). Alleluia and praise the LORD. There are a few "holidays" that surround that time of year, namely, "Guy Fox" day, "All Saints" day, "Día de Muertos" or Day of the dead, and the infamous "All Hallows Eve", as of the date of writing this book in 2019 A.D.. You can look into each of them yourself, but let's consider them all, in general. They are all associated with death, the dead, ghostly spirits, and in some circumstances some sort of resurrection or resurrections of the dead. All of which are topics, mentioned throughout the Bible. Also, I should say that remembering the deceased, especially if they were a godly example during their lifetime, is not necessarily wrong, but worshipping them and trying to consult with them maybe an entirely different situation (Ex. 3:6, 1 Chr. 29:18). Alleluia and praise the LORD. Amen and Amen.

Now, let us consider a "Holy Day" in the Old Testament, also mentioned in the New Testament; stepping forth in faith, I will attempt to relate it to the time of the year traditionally known as "Halloween". The day in question is related to the fall feast days called the "Feast of Tabernacles" in particular it is the "Last Great Day" of this festival (Lev. 23:39, John 7:37). To expand on this idea, the book of Revelation speaks of this day in greater detail as being the final day, the Great White Throne

---

[16] https://en.wikipedia.org/wiki/Thanksgiving#In_the_United_States, retrieved 18/04/2022

Judgement, etc. (Rev. 20:11-15). It is the day when all whom have ever lived here on this earth, will be resurrected to either receive eternal life or eternal death, God's Final Judgment on this world and all whom have ever lived in it (Dan. 12:2, Matt. 25:34, 41, 46; 2 Peter 3:7, Rev. 11:18, Rev. 20:11-15, etc.). This day was also spoken of in greater detail in chapter six of this book and in other books I have written. But the Holy Bible of God ought to be the first and really only place we need to go to, outside the Holy Spirit of God, for knowledge and understanding of these teachings. Nevertheless, is it any wonder that Halloween is so close in the calendar year to the "Last Great Day", mentioned in the Bible, and has everything to do with spirit beings, ghosts, the "living dead", etc.? Nevertheless, regardless of the truth of Halloween and its origins, we should always put our daily life into proper perspective. As I had said earlier, we serve a living God, and He is all about life. Consider this when you do your trick or treating or join in gatherings that celebrate that time of year, as of the date of writing this book in 2019 A.D.. And seek the one Ghost that will give you all of the answers and comfort you are looking for and will ever need, the Holy Ghost (John 14:26). God has a plan for us; He has always had a plan for us and will always have a plan for us (Jer. 29:11, 2 Peter 3:9). Let Him, through Christ into your plans for that "season" of celebration and your daily life, in general, and remember that with God, the Father, and His only begotten Son, Jesus Christ of Nazareth, through His Holy Spirit, we have eternal life. Alleluia and praise the LORD. Amen and Amen.

Feast of Dedication and Christmas

Jesus and the Feast of Dedication; Hanukkah (John 10:22, 23). This could very well point to Jesus Christ's conception by the Holy Spirit, in the virgin, Mary, espoused to Joseph, both of the House of David (Matt. 1, Luke 3). Jesus kept it (John 10:22, 23). In Jewish writing and celebration, the Jews celebrate a holiday called, Hanukkah, during this time of year. If you do not already know, this holiday is about a miracle that took place over 2100 years ago, just before Christ's physical time here on earth, as of the date of writing this book in 2019 A.D.. The holiday is about a miracle that is explained in Maccabees time, not a "canonized" Biblical text, but as the account goes, the Jews were fighting against the Roman and Greek governing bodies, namely Antiochus of Syria, and did not have enough oil to sustain the ritual lamps. Miraculously, the lamps stayed lit for the eight days required, until they could make more oil to supply its burning.[17] There is much more to this account and note, it is not "canonized" Bible teaching strictly speaking, but miracles happen every day. So no judgements made from my point of view. Jesus' conception by the Holy Spirit in the virgin, Mary, espoused to Joseph, was highly likely during that time in December of 5 B.C.. Haggai 2:18 and 19 say, "Consider now from this day and upward, from the four and twentieth day of the ninth *month, even* from the day that the foundation of the LORD's temple was laid, consider *it.* Is the seed yet in the barn? yea, as yet the vine, and the fig tree, and the pomegranate, and the olive tree, hath not brought forth: from this day will I bless *you.*". This may be prophetic in pointing to the conception of Jesus Christ of Nazareth on the 24th day of the ninth month of the Hebrew calendar. Miraculously this works out to be the 24th of Kislev and in 5 B.C., it is actually the 24th of December!!!!!!! Which is also the eve of the Feast of Dedication, mentioned above, Hanukkah (John 10:22, 23)! So here we have incredible evidence, if this interpretation is true, that indeed Jesus was conceived on the eve of the day we celebrate as the day of Christ's birth and in 5 B.C., the eve of Hanukkah, that celebrates the miraculous burning of light, and Jesus is that true light, a lamp unto our feet (Matt. 1:18-25, John 1:1-9, 8:12). Alleluia

---

[17] https://en.wikipedia.org/wiki/Hanukkah#Books_of_Maccabees, retrieved 18/04/2022

and praise the LORD. A note should be made to understand, that a person is a living being at the moment of conception. Alleluia and praise the LORD. Amen and Amen. And I should also note, that the Roman date was determined using a calendar date converter from; http://www.cgsf.org/dbeattie/calendar/?roman=5+B.C., retrieved 08/01/2018. I checked with another calendar date converting website and it gave me an answer of the equivalent of 3 December, 5 B.C., https://calcuworld.com/calendar-calculators/hebrew-calendar-converter/, retrieved 08/01/2018. I should also note, that I have used the former calendar date converting website, cgsf.org, for most of my other calculations and conversions for dating various events surrounding Jesus' life and some other events mentioned in the Bible. So keep this in mind. I have **no reason** to believe, cgsf.org, is inaccurate, although as the Bible says, "Prove all things; hold fast that which is good." (1 Thess. 5:21). So I will leave it up to you to decide, for certain, for yourself, what the truth of the matter is. Alleluia and praise the LORD. Amen and Amen.

Also, upon further investigation using skyviewcafe.com, settings to Jerusalem at 11am, 24th September, 5 B.C., accidentally, there is in the sky the constellation of Virgo, the virgin, with Venus the "Morning Star" and the Sun, very close to the womb and/or one hand of Virgo. If this is not a sign and wonder in the stars of the miraculous conception of Christ in the blessed virgin, Mary, I do not know what is; albeit three months before the preferred date of Mary's conception, but close to the date of the feast of trumpets, which was in 5 B.C., Oct. 2nd, one week after the sign, which will be spoken about more below and was spoken of in chapter five of this book. With Virgo's head and/or one hand reaching, depending on how you interpret the constellation, toward the constellation of Leo, again, pointing back to Jesus Christ of Nazareth, as the Lion of the tribe of Judah, King of Israel, and Saviour of the whole world (Rev. 5:5). Alleluia and praise the LORD. This was again an accidental find, thinking that I might find the constellation based on some other people's interpretations on December 24th, I typed in 09/24/5 B.C., forgetting that I had to convert to the Roman dating system. I will say, for argument sake though; that this could be a prophetic sign of what was to come in the months ahead. Also, as Barry Carter had warned me, the software used to calculate the constellations and planetary movements are not perfect either. Which, as will be mentioned, goes along with the scriptural indication of the same, in the book of Job 15:15, it says, "…the heavens are not clean in his sight." and Job 25:5, says, "…the stars are not pure in his sight.". Nevertheless, they are to be for signs and seasons and days and years (Gen. 1:14, 15). After this, I did search the correct date of December 24th, 5 B.C. and found Mars and Pluto near Virgo. If you are willing to go the extra mile with me, I will do a brief interpretation of this, if truthful, as well (Matt. 5:41). Pluto, apparently has an affiliation with Hades, in mythology, https://en.wikipedia.org/wiki/Pluto#Name, retrieved 09/01/2018. And Jesus was given the keys to hell and death, by overcoming the evils of this world and Satan, in Jesus' lifetime here on earth, including fleeing into Egypt as a young child with His parents from evil king Herod, whom sought to kill the young Jesus (Matt. 2:13, Rev. 1:18, Rev. 12). Also, the planet, Mars, in mythology, is affiliated with the god of war, and the male symbol in general, https://en.wikipedia.org/wiki/Mars#In_culture, retrieved 09/01/2018. Jesus is, "…I AM…", and in the Old Testament, God proclaims Himself to be a "…man of war…" (Ex. 3:14, 15:3; John 8:58). And in the book of Revelation, it speaks of Jesus, The Word of God, wearing a vesture dipped in blood coming with His army of heaven dressed in white and on white horses (Rev. 19:13, 14). So this all may indeed be prophetic of things that have happened, as well as for things to come, but ultimately, we must still consider the innocent child, Jesus, His humble, meek and life giving servant like earthly ministry for God, the Father, to all of us during

His thirty three and a half years here on earth, dying on the cross for the forgiveness of our sins at Passover in 31 A.D., He was buried and He arose the third day to give us the promise and hope of eternal life in His Holy name. Alleluia and praise the LORD. Amen and Amen.

One reference that Barry Carter gave me during our brief but helpful conversation; albeit, I had stumbled across the reference a week earlier, is askelm.com. This person, Ernest L. Martin, has written extensively on the subject of Jesus' birth, amongst other biblical topics. He addresses the prophecy, although some had already happened, of John's revelation, namely chapter twelve of the book of Revelation, in the Holy Bible of God. This, he indicates, had prophetic significance to Jesus' birth. Namely, the verse of the woman in heaven, he references Virgo, clothed with the Sun (Rev. 12:1). This is in regards to interpreting the sign of Christ's birth, as the Sun moves through the constellation of Virgo from head to toe, the sun seems actually to exit the body of Virgo, right around the time of, the feast of trumpets; another sign of Jesus Christ of Nazareth's physical birth in the fall season time. He suggested this happened in around August 27 to September 15 in 3 B.C., http://www.askelm.com/star/star006.htm, retrieved 09/01/2018, which according to skyviewcafe.com is true. But it also happened around the same time in 4 B.C., as well. The main difference between these two years seems to be that Mars is present between Virgo and Leo in 3 B.C., and Venus is present between Virgo and Leo in 4 B.C.. This could be interpreted as the difference between a waring king being born; and a gentle, meek and humble king and Messiah being born, which the latter is what the Bible describes the fleshly, Immanuel, God with us, Jesus Christ of Nazareth, as being (Matt. 1:29, 11:29). Venus also is a sign for femininity, which would describe generally; tenderness, gentleness, and other generally female qualities, https://en.wikipedia.org/wiki/Venus#In_culture, retrieved 09/01/2018. But in the "bigger" picture, this may also help fulfill a prophecy in the Old Testament that says, "Set thee up waymarks, make thee high heaps: set thine heart toward the highway, *even* the way *which* thou wentest: turn again, O virgin of Israel, turn again to these thy cities. How long wilt thou go about, O thou backsliding daughter? for the LORD hath created a new thing in the earth, **A woman shall compass a man.**" (Jer. 31:21, 22). Of course, Jesus lived with His parents and submitted to His mother and father's authority; He healed and forgave multiple women, one of whom the authorities were ready to stone for adultery, and He was also ministered to through them, from time to time, and last, He entrusted His mother to the disciple John, at Jesus' crucifixion; Jesus also referred to wisdom as a "her" (Matt. 8:15, 11:19; Mark 15:40, 41; Luke 2:41-52, 8:3; John 8:1-11, 19:26, 27). That being said, as the Holy Bible says, "...God is no respecter of persons..."; male, female or otherwise, we are all one in Christ Jesus of Nazareth (Acts 10:34). Alleluia and praise the LORD. Amen and Amen. This is another good example of why, as truth seekers, we need to diligently and prayerfully search and consider the scriptures and any other references we use, if we are going to use them, to prove what indeed the truth is. As Jesus said, "...the truth shall make you free." (John 8:32). I am certainly not judging Mr. Martin, as the Bible says, "...precept upon precept; ...line upon line; here a little, *and* there a little..." and "...we know in part, and we prophecy in part." (Isa. 28:10, 1 Cor. 13:9). But we need to indeed, put Christ Jesus of Nazareth, first in our life. Alleluia and praise the LORD. My interpretations are just that, if they are correct, than to God be the Glory! If they are wrong, God still receives the glory, and hopefully, at best, I will be forgiven and the works will be burned up at some point in time (1 Cor. 3:15). No matter, I will continue with these interpretations of the opening days and years of Jesus' earthly life, continuing with more proof using the time of conception and birth of John the Baptist to work from. Alleluia and praise the LORD. Amen and Amen.

John the Baptist was conceived, in Elizabeth, the wife of Zecharias, six months prior to Jesus' miraculous conception in the virgin, Mary, espoused to Joseph (Matt. 1:18-25, Luke 1:24-27). Knowingly or not, "Saint Jean Baptiste" day is celebrated at that time of year, June 24th. Some confirmation of this conception date, is because the Bible says that Zecharias, John's father, was of the course of Abijah, a Levite, which would have had his service at the temple in May/June; he was of the eighth course, a course serving each week, and all priests served at the week of Passover and Pentecost according to some online references (1 Ch. 24:10, Luke 1:5, 8, 9). So John would have likely been conceived shortly after Zecharias returned home unto his wife after his service was finished (Luke 1:23, 24). Both references I found on the topic, suggest that he was conceived after Zecharias would have been done his service in the temple just after the middle of June in 5 B.C.. Using Christ's conception on the 24th of December 5 B.C., and working six months back would bring us to the 24th of June in 5 B.C., for John's conception. See http://biblelight.net/ sukkoth.htm, retrieved 03/01/2018, and http://www.sabbath.org/index.cfm/fuseaction/Library.sr/ CT/ARTB/k/568/When-Was-Jesus-Born.htm, retrieved 03/01/2018, for some confirmation of the approximate dating of John and Christ's conceptions and births. Jesus' birth nine months after His Holy Spirit conception in the virgin, Mary, espoused to Joseph, on 24th December in 5 B.C., would be at about 1 Tishri/Ethanim in 4 B.C., which is in around September, October depending on the year (Lev. 23:23-25, Matt. 1:18-25). The reference immediately above, at sabbath.org, suggests a range of dates that includes 1 Tishri/Ethanim in 4 B.C.. So, that is highly likely the time of Jesus Christ of Nazareth's earthly birth, as mentioned in chapter five. For those interested in starry signs, using skyviewcafe.com, and settings of Jerusalem at 4am on September 22nd in 4 B.C.; it turns out that the constellation Leo, Jesus is known as the lion of the tribe of Judah; and the "Morningstar" Venus, Jesus is also known as the Morningstar; are rather close together at this time, this indeed could be a sign of the Messiah's birth date (Rev. 5:5, 22:16). Two years later, at 1 Tishri/Ethanim in 2 B.C., the "king planet", Jupiter, and the constellation, Leo, are in the same area of the sky, using skyviewcafe.com again, settings of Jerusalem at 4am on September 29th in 2 B.C.. This could be another sign of the Messiah, as the Lion of the tribe of Judah and King of the Jews as the wise men recognized Him as, likely at that time of year (Matt. 2:2, Rev. 5:5). The wise men from the east, likely saw the conjunction of Venus, Jupiter and Regulus earlier, on August 17th in 2 B.C., giving them time to travel to Jerusalem and then onto Bethlehem in time to recognize Jesus, likely on His second birthday, as "King of the Jews" (Matt. 2:2).[18] I should say that I owe credit to Barry Carter, mentioned in the reference appendix and above, for his initial work on the August 17th conjunction and a brief conversation where I was given a reference to skyviewcafe.com to search the matter further. Proof positive of Jesus' commands, "Ask, and it shall be given you; seek, and ye shall find…" (Matt. 7:7). Alleluia and praise the LORD. Amen and Amen.

Next; Joseph, Mary and young Jesus, moved to Egypt for a time to get away from the evil Herod, whom heard the sign from the wise men, that a king had been born within the previous two years (Matt. 2:13-15). Joseph, Mary and young Jesus fled shortly after the wise men came to them; and if my dating is correct, Joseph, Mary and young Jesus, likely would have left shortly after the feast of trumpets in 2 B.C., around September 29th. It is interesting that the feast of tabernacles is just fourteen days later, as this was done partially in remembrance of the wilderness journey of the Israelites (Lev. 23:33-44). I do not think that it would be a coincidence, that the young child, Jesus, and His parents,

---

[18] https://astronomy.stackexchange.com/questions/11456/has-the-conjunction-between-venus-jupiter-and-regulus-only-occurred-twice-in-2, retrieved 03/01/2018

would have to flee to "sukkot", tabernacle, in Egypt for a certain amount of time, until it was safe to return to the land of Israel (Matt. 2:13-15). This was also prophesied of in the Old Testament, and Jesus fulfilled it well (Hos. 11:1). Matthew 2:14 and 15 say, "When he arose, he took the young child and his mother by night, and departed into Egypt: And was there until the death of Herod: that it might be fulfilled which was spoken of the Lord by the prophet, saying, Out of Egypt have I called my son.". Last, there seems to be some strong indication that king Herod died in later winter of 1 B.C. (Matt. 2:19, 20). Josephus, a Jewish historian, recorded Herod dying after a lunar eclipse and a fast, but before the annual Passover (Zech. 8:19). These references can be found in the writing of Josephus, in Antiquities 17.6.4, 17.9.3 and Jewish wars 2.1.3, available on the internet at, https://www.ccel.org/ccel/josephus/complete.toc.html, retrieved 08/01/2018. Some historians have suggested anywhere from 4 B.C. to 1 B.C. for the death of king Herod. See the following website, https://www.biblicalarchaeology.org/daily/people-cultures-in-the-bible/jesus-historical-jesus/herods-death-jesus-birth-and-a-lunar-eclipse/, retrieved 08/01/2018. But as said, there seems to be some strong indication that he died in early 1 B.C., http://www.askelm.com/star/star011.htm, retrieved 09/01/2018. There was a fast, January 6th in 1 B.C., and a lunar eclipse on January 10th in 1 B.C. and Passover would have followed just over three months later on the 14th of Nisan, the 7th of April 1 B.C. (Lev. 23:5). This would confirm God's swift judgement on those whom hurt His people, if indeed Jesus and His parents fled to Egypt, a few months earlier, in the fall of 2 B.C. (Matt. 2:13-21). I would suggest this is highly likely the truth of the matter. If this is the case, I would suggest, Jesus and His parents came back out of Egypt, sometime in early 1 B.C. (Matt. 2:19-23). Possibly in order to celebrate Passover in their native land, Israel, and so that Jesus could be raise up a child of Israel, and eventually be confirmed as King of the Jews, and the Saviour of the whole world as a grown man at Passover in 31 A.D. (Luke 2:41-52, John 19:19). Not only this, but He died on the cross for the forgiveness of our sins, He was buried and He arose the third day to give us the hope and promise of eternal life in His Holy name. Alleluia and praise the LORD. Amen and Amen.

It has been suggested that Christmas was a result of the Roman church attempting to reconcile pagan, sun worship, and the so called solstices, with the belief of Christianity (Ps. 19).[19] This subject is gone into, in more depth, in my book, "Origin of Mankind"; essentially, it speaks of Israel's initial rebellion after coming into the "promised land" in about 1400 B.C. (Jud. 18, 1 Kings 12:26-33). And the Bible does speak of the rebellious house of Israel worshipping a "star", a created thing, rather than the true God, God, the Father of us all in Christ Jesus of Nazareth, whom are Spirit first and foremost (Amos 5:26, Acts 7:43). In prophetic blessings and in the book of Judges, the Danites were to "…leap from Bashan." in Northern Israel; they and other Israelite captives, later on, likely became the Greeks, Romans and onto the western empires of today (Deut. 33:22, Jud. 18, 2 Kings 15:29, 17; Ps. 68:15-23). Psalm 68:22 and 23 say, "The Lord said, I will bring again from Bashan, I will bring *my people* again from the depths of the sea: That thy foot may be dipped in the blood of *thine* enemies, *and* the tongue of thy dogs in the same.". This has and is being fulfilled in Jesus Christ of Nazareth, with the preaching of the gospel of the kingdom of God, and Christ dying on the cross for the forgiveness of our sins at Passover in 31 A.D., He was buried and arose the third day to give us the hope and promise of eternal life in His Holy name. The "…lost sheep of the house of Israel." are essentially the western people of today, whom throughout the centuries have migrated from where our ancient ancestors dwelt, in Israel proper (Matt. 10:6). Of course, we have had other migrations of other peoples since then, but generally the Judaeo-Christian rooted people of the west

---

[19] https://rcg.org/realtruth/articles/101129-002-religion.html, retrieved 18/04/2022

are the "...lost sheep of the house of Israel." (Matt. 10:6). This prophecy of feet dipped in blood is twofold; one is that we will have rule over our enemies, even our dogs will. But in the Bible, dogs can also be certain types of people; male prostitutes and prophets are also considered dogs (Deut. 23:18, Isa. 56:10, 11). Considering whom Jesus was and whom He died for, this is a very descriptive, if understood this way, example of whom Jesus died for on the cross. His feet were bloodied by His own blood, not someone else's, but that blood was shed because of the enemy, us, our sins most namely (Ps. 14, 53). And He is a prophet, and He took the sins of all of mankind upon Himself, that includes the sins of false prophets, prophets, male prostitutes, idolaters, etc.. This is why the message of the cross of Jesus Christ of Nazareth is so important. He has forgiven us all of our sins, and has extended to us the gift of eternal life for all whom believe on His Holy name. Alleluia and praise the LORD. Amen and Amen.

I write about these things because Jesus said, "...the truth shall make you free." (John 8:32). I should also say, that this is certainly an interpretation, and I actually started many of these date "assumptions" surrounding Christ's earthly life working backward from His crucifixion at Passover in 31 A.D., to fit the rest of the puzzle together; and even this information did not come to me in a dream or vision, it originated from the church of God that I was attending early on in my conversion in 2010 A.D.. The other thing I should say, is that doing all of this research, namely regarding the "stars", which is not much information in the end, but helps put the pieces of the bigger puzzle together more fitly; is that in Job 25:5 it says, "...the stars are not pure in his sight.". This is likely part of the reason why in my references and others on the internet and elsewhere, in general, there are so many different conclusions for the date of Christ's birth, when the wise men visited Him, and the like. Plus, ultimately, God takes full responsibility for people's failures, which brings me back to the point of all of this, which is, Jesus Christ of Nazareth dying on the cross for the forgiveness of our sins, spilling His Holy and righteous blood, as a sinless man, taking our sins upon Himself. He was buried and He arose the third day to give us the hope and promise of eternal life in His Holy name. Alleluia and praise the LORD. Amen and Amen. But no matter the truth of this. God has sovereign authority over all of these things. He calls us out of the world, and into His truth; that is, Jesus Christ of Nazareth. God will guide you by His Holy Spirit in you, as to how you keep any other "feasts", outside of what feasts God calls us to keep, mentioned in the Holy Bible of God (Lev. 23). The book of Acts may be a good place to start in understanding how to relate to "gentile" beliefs and how to relate to others. Namely, Jesus Christ of Nazareth, said simply and plainly, "Therefore all things whatsoever ye would that men should do to you, do ye even so to them: for this is the law and the prophets." (Matt. 7:12). Psalm 119:126 says, "*It is* time for *thee,* LORD, to work: *for* they have made void thy law.". This is the reality of all of this stuff. We need to trust in Jesus Christ of Nazareth and the work He has done for us on the cross, spilling His Holy and righteous blood, for the forgiveness of our sins, His death on the cross, His burial and His resurrection three days later for the hope and promise of eternal life in His Holy name, as our cornerstone in all of this (Eph. 2:20-22). We need faith in God, through Christ Jesus of Nazareth. Alleluia and praise the LORD. Remember that Jesus Christ of Nazareth came full of grace and truth and it is by His grace that we are saved (John 1:14, Eph. 2:8, 9). He did not come to condemn the world, but to save it (John 3:17). So we ought also to live and walk in the grace of God all the days of our life, and forever more in the world to come, by the forgiveness of our sins and the promise of eternal life in the life, death on the cross for the forgiveness of our sins, burial and resurrection, three days later, unto eternal life of Jesus Christ of Nazareth. Alleluia and praise the LORD. Amen and Amen.

First of the Hebrew Calendar Year and New Year's Day

In appendix A, I mentioned the Hebrew Calendar, as well as I spoke of it in chapter one of this book. But the question may remain, when is the first day of the New Year? According to the Bible it is 1 Nisan, which usually lands on sometime in the spring, March or April, depending on the year (Est. 3:7). But traditionally we celebrate the New Year as January 1st. So where did this dating system come from, if not from the Bible directly? Well, I will say, I am not an expert in this; but I will tell you what I have found, regarding this dating system. It seems that in the 6th century, a man named Dionysus Exiguus, is credited with the current roman numeral calendar system we use, Anno Domini, meaning "in the year of the Lord", https://en.wikipedia.org/wiki/Anno_Domini, retrieved 08/01/2018. This is the suggested reason why there is no year zero, because the roman numeral system has no zero in it. I know that there are at least two calendar systems within the more recent system; that is, the Julian calendar and the Gregorian calendar. Today, we traditionally use the Gregorian calendar system, as mentioned in chapter one of this book. This is just speculation at this time, but I would suggest that traditionally people may very well have thought that Jesus was born at this time of year. This may very well be the reason why the calendar system is dated as such. Of course, Jesus' life was, no doubt, paramount in affecting the life of all inhabitants here on earth, even those whom were born before Christ, the Saviour of us all, in the flesh. Upon further research into Dionysus Exiguus, a Wikipedia article about him does seem to suggest he dated Christ's birth to be in around 1 A.D., https://en.wikipedia.org/wiki/Dionysius_Exiguus#Anno_Domini, retrieved 08/01/2018. There is also some other more political reasons given for his desire to change the calendar system, which apparently has something to do with Roman Emperor Diocletian, circa 284 B.C. and the persecution of Christians, https://en.wikipedia.org/wiki/Era_of_Martyrs, retrieved 08/01/2018.

Nevertheless, as suggested earlier, evidences seem to suggest and I would argue quite accurately, that Jesus was conceived in December of 5 B.C., likely on the 24th and born in September of 4 B.C, likely on the 22nd, at the feast of trumpets (Lev. 23:23-25, Hag. 2:18, 19; Luke 2:4-18). I am not suggesting that we need to change the calendar system as it stands, quite the opposite actually. Certainly, the Bible in Genesis suggests that the sun, and the moon and the stars were created for signs, and for seasons, and for days and years, and this has not changed (Gen. 1:14, 15). And for one reason or another we have come to keep time according to the Anno Domini system, at least in the "bigger picture", but we must not forget that, in Christ Jesus of Nazareth, we have freedom (John 8:32). We have freedom, through Jesus Christ of Nazareth, from this world and its ways. Jesus said of Himself, "...My kingdom is not of this world..." (John 18:36). He also said, that if our righteousness does not exceed that of the scribes and Pharisees, we are not fit for the kingdom of God (Matt. 5:20). But also we must remember that Jesus Christ of Nazareth came, "...full of grace and truth." (John 1:14). This means, that it is not by our own works that we are saved, but by the work of Christ on the cross, that we are saved. Alleluia and praise the LORD. It is not by celebrating this day or that day, but as the apostle, Paul, says, "Rejoice in the Lord alway: *and* again I say, Rejoice." (Phil. 4:4). Alleluia and praise the LORD. We need to remember in the midst of all of these feasts, and celebrations, and worldly temptations, in general; that Christ came as a meek and humble servant of God (Matt. 11:29). Not as a dictator with wrath, but as a man whom was willing to give up His own life for us, so that all whom believe in Him will not perish, but will receive eternal life (John 3:16). Alleluia and praise the LORD. So now you have a choice to make. Whom are you going to follow, the Creator, in Christ Jesus of Nazareth's Holy name, Immanuel,

God with us, or the world and your own fleshly desires? I leave the choice up to you. Alleluia and praise the LORD. Amen and Amen.

Conclusion

Last, keep in your mind why you do the things you do, and why you celebrate the "feasts" you do. If there is a positive, God given relationship, then no harm no foul (Rom. 14:4-5). If there are some negative ideas you may associate with them, address them and turn them into positives. It is only a handful of days at most, out of the year. Make them joyful ones. As the Bible says, "Rejoice in the Lord alway…" (Phil. 4:4). And on a purely physical level, it is always a good idea to refrain from overindulgence of candy, food and/or alcohol for your health's sake and with alcohol, the health of those around you, because of irresponsible driving, etc.. So, as the saying goes, do your best to "keep Christ in Christmas" and any other day you celebrate Him, and God, the Father, through His Holy Spirit, given to us. This year and in the years to come, until the whole world knows Christ reigns as King of Kings and Lord of Lords. Alleluia and praise the LORD. Amen and Amen.

The song that seems to be traditionally song, among others at the celebration of Jesus Christ of Nazareth's coming into this world as a Holy Spirit conceived child in the virgin, Mary, espoused to Joseph, is, "Oh, come, oh, come, Emmanuel, And ransom captive Israel…"; Translated: John Neal, 1818-66. Jesus Christ of Nazareth, Jesus Christ Immanuel of Nazareth, is Emmanuel (Isa. 7:14, Matt. 1:18-25). He has come in the flesh (John 1:1-3). He preached the gospel, the good news of the kingdom of God (Mark 1:14). He healed the sick, blind, and lame, cast out devils and forgave us our sins (Matt. 4:23). He died on the cross to show us how much He loves us, for the forgiveness of our sins, in place of us, for our transgressions, our iniquity. He died for us on the cross. But not only this, He was buried and He arose the third day to give us all the hope and promise of eternal life in His Holy name. Alleluia and praise the LORD. Amen and Amen.

Ezekiel 20:25 and 26 say, "Wherefore I gave them also statutes *that were* not good, and judgements whereby they should not live; And I polluted them in their own gifts, in that they caused to pass through *the fire* all that openeth the womb, that I might make them desolate, to the end that they might know that I *am* the LORD.". Christmas and Easter, the empires claiming Sunday, the first day of the week, to be a day of rest instead of Saturday, the seventh day of the week, eating unclean meats, celebrating birthdays and other "heathen" like festivals (Gen. 2:2, 3; Lev. 11, Job 1:4, 5). God's commands of the Bible are truth. Jesus Christ of Nazareth is the truth. That being said, Jesus came full of "…grace and truth."; not just truth (John 1:14). God is merciful, forgiving, longsuffering and He loves us in Christ Jesus of Nazareth's Holy name (Gal. 5:22, 23). He says to love the enemy and pray for those that persecute us (Matt. 5:44). He said we would be able to pick up serpents and drink any deadly thing and not be hurt (Mark. 16:18). Ultimately, Jesus Christ of Nazareth, came into this world, conceived by the Holy Spirit in and born to the virgin, Mary, espoused to Joseph (Matt. 1:18-25). He was raised, a child of Israel, of the tribe of Judah, with brothers and sisters (Matt. 13:55, 56; Luke 2:41-52). He ministered for three and a half years, starting at about the age of thirty (Luke 3:21-23). And at Passover in 31 A.D., He died on the cross for the forgiveness of our sins, shedding His Holy and righteous blood, He was buried and He arose the third day to give us all the hope and promise of eternal life in His Holy name. Alleluia and praise the LORD. Amen and Amen.

APPENDIX C

Jubile, Land Sabbath and the Last Great Day

Introduction

Before I had ever considered writing or had made any detailed plans to minister, what I believe to be the gospel of God, I had an experience at work, while I was employed in the engineering field, soon after I was released from the military. You can take out of this account of my experience what you will. However, I was in my boss's office one day, talking to him about some design drawings I was working on, when out of the corner of my right eye, I saw some small light moving, it moved directly toward the power bar used to power the boss's computer and other office equipment, and then a spark came out of the power bar. I will openly admit, I have seen strange things with my eyes in the past, but nothing like this. And I suppose since God first revealed Himself to me, namely in a vision in the night, I have been more aware of experiencing life in ways I had never expected nor thought of before. Nevertheless, this is exactly how God seems to work, and not only that, as we place our trust in Him, He will reveal more to us. A perfect example is in Moses; first, God revealed Himself to Moses in a burning bush on Mount Horeb (Ex. 3:2). Then the miracles and responsibilities grew to the point, that God caused the Red Sea to go back by a strong east wind all night, and the sea was made dry land and divided, after Moses stretched his hand over it (Ex. 14:21). And the miracles of God continued throughout the wilderness journey, and in the remainder of the Old Testament into the New Testament with Jesus Christ of Nazareth's miraculous conception in the virgin, Mary, and other miracles He and His followers have done since then, in the name of the Almighty God of Israel and of all of mankind (Matt. 1:18-25). Alleluia and praise the LORD. Amen and Amen. My point here, is to share, that God is indeed a God of miracles, and a God whose ways are higher than our own (Isa. 55:8, 9). He is also a God of abundance. Obedience to God, brings a blessing we cannot contain (1 Kings 8:27). The plowman will overtake the reaper there will be so much abundance (Amos 9:13). A cup overflowing (Ps. 23:5). Jesus came to give us life and life more abundantly (John 10:10). Alleluia and praise the LORD. Amen and Amen. With this all being said, read on to learn more about some of these commands regarding rest and release from all burdens, and what these commands may prophetically speak of for things to come. Alleluia and praise the LORD. Amen and Amen.

Jubile

Leviticus 25:8-55 says, "And thou shalt number seven sabbaths of years unto thee, seven times seven years; and the space of the seven sabbaths of years shall be unto thee forty and nine years. Then shalt thou cause the trumpet of the jubile to sound on the tenth *day* of the seventh month, in the day of atonement shall ye make the trumpet sound throughout all your land. And ye shall hallow the fiftieth year, and proclaim liberty throughout *all* the land unto all the inhabitants thereof: it shall be a jubile unto you; and ye shall return every man unto his possession, and ye shall return every man unto his family. A jubile shall that fiftieth year be unto you: ye shall not sow, neither reap that which groweth of itself in it, nor gather *the grapes* in it of thy vine undressed. For it *is* the jubile; it shall be holy unto you: ye shall eat the increase thereof out of the field. In the year of this jubile ye shall return every man unto his possession. And if thou sell ought unto thy neighbor, or buyest *ought* of thy neighbour's hand, ye shall not oppress one another: According to the number of years after the jubile thou shalt buy of thy neighbour, *and* according unto the number of years of the fruits he shall sell unto thee: According to the multitude of years thou shalt increase the price thereof, and according to the fewness of years thou shalt diminish the price of it: for *according* to the number *of the years* of the fruits doth he sell unto thee. Ye shall not therefore oppress one another; but thou shalt fear thy God:for I *am* the LORD your God.

Wherefore ye shall do my statutes, and keep my judgments, and do them; and ye shall dwell in the land in safety. And the land shall yield her fruit, and ye shall eat your fill, and dwell therein in safety. And if ye shall say, What shall we eat the seventh year? behold, we shall not sow, nor gather in our increase: Then I will command my blessing upon you in the sixth year, and it shall bring forth fruit for three years. And ye shall sow the eighth year, and eat *yet* of old fruit until the ninth year; until her fruits come in ye shall eat *of* the old *store*.

The land shall not be sold for ever: for the land *is* mine, for ye *are* strangers and sojourners with me. And in all the land of your possession ye shall grant a redemption for the land.

If thy brother be waxen poor, and hath sold away *some* of his possession, and if any of his kin come to redeem it, then shall he redeem that which his brother sold. And if the man have none to redeem it, and himself be able to redeem it; Then let him count the years of the sale thereof, and restore the overplus unto the man to whom he sold it; that he may return unto his possession. But if he be not able to restore *it* to him, then that which is sold shall remain in the hand of him that hath bought it until the year of jubile: and in the jubile it shall go out, and he shall return unto his possession.

And if a man sell a dwelling house in a walled city, then he may redeem it within a whole year after it is sold; *within* a full year may he redeem it. And if it be not redeemed within the space of a full year, then the house that *is* in the walled city shall be established for ever to him that bought it throughout his generations: it shall not go out in the jubile. But the houses of the villages which have no wall round about them shall be counted as the fields of the country: they may be redeemed, and they shall go out in the jubile. Notwithstanding the cities of the Levites, *and* the houses of the cities of their possession, may the Levites redeem at any time. And if a man purchase of the Levites, then the house that was sold, and the city of his possession, shall go out in *the year of* jubile: for the houses of the cities of the Levites *are* their possession among the children of Israel. But the field of the suburbs of their cities may not be sold; for it *is* their perpetual possession.

And if thy brother be waxen poor, and fallen in decay with thee; then thou shalt relieve him: yea, *though he be* a stranger, or a sojourner; that he may live with thee. Take thou no usury of him, or increase: but fear thy God; that thy brother may live with thee. Thou shalt not give him thy money upon usury, nor lend him thy victuals for increase. I *am* the LORD your God, which brought you forth out of the land of Egypt, to give you the land of Canaan, *and* to be your God.

And if thy brother *that dwelleth* by thee be waxen poor, and be sold unto thee; thou shalt not compel him to serve as a bondservant: *But* as an hired servant, *and* as a sojourner, he shall be with thee, *and* shall serve thee unto the year of jubile. And *then* shall he depart from thee, *both* he and his children with him, and shall return unto his own family, and unto the possession of his fathers shall he return.

For they *are* my servants, which I brought forth out of the land of Egypt: they shall not be sold as bondmen. Thou shalt not rule over him with rigour; but shalt fear thy God. Both thy bondmen, and thy bondmaids, which thou shalt have, *shall be* of the heathen that are round about you; of them shall ye buy bondmen and bondmaids. Moreover of the children of the strangers that do sojourn among you, of them shall ye buy, and of their families that *are* with you, which they begat in your land: and they shall be your possession. And ye shall take them as an inheritance for your children after you, to inherit *them for* a possession; they shall be your bondmen for ever: but over your brethren the children of Israel, ye shall not rule one over another with rigour.

And if a sojourner or stranger wax rich by thee, and thy brother *that dwelleth* by him wax poor, and sell himself unto the stranger *or* sojourner by thee, or to the stock of the stranger's family: After that he is sold he may be redeemed again; one of his brethren may redeem him: Either his uncle, or his uncle's son, may redeem him, or *any* that is nigh of kin unto him of his family may redeem him; or if he be able, he may redeem himself. And he shall reckon with him that bought him from the year that he was sold to him unto the year of jubile: and the price of his sale shall be according unto the number of years, according to the time of an hired servant shall it be with him. If *there be* yet many years *behind,* according unto them he shall give again the price of his redemption out of the money that he was bought for. And if there remain but few years unto the year of jubile, then he shall count with him, *and* according unto his years shall he give him again the price of his redemption. *And* as a yearly hired servant shall he be with him: *and the other* shall not rule with rigour over him in thy sight. And if he be not redeemed in these *years,* then he shall go out in the year of jubile, *both* he, and his children with him. For unto me the children of Israel *are* servants; they *are* my servants whom I brought forth out of the land of Egypt: I *am* the LORD your God.".

Ministry work, according to the Old Testament, begins at age 50 (Num. 8:25, 26). Pentecost is 50 days from the first Sabbath after Passover (Lev. 23:15-22). Jesus started His ministry at about the age of 30 (Luke 3:23). He was even chastised for not being fifty years old at one point; albeit, this was in regards to Abraham seeing Jesus' earthly life, likely in vision (John 8:56, 57). Nevertheless, Jesus Christ of Nazareth is the Messiah, the true Minister, healer, forgiver, and redeemer of all of mankind; regardless of our age or socioeconomic status. That is, "…God is no respecter of persons…" (Acts 10:34). Praise the LORD, God, the Father, Almighty, and His only begotten Son, Jesus Christ of Nazareth, with His Holy Spirit. Alleluia and praise the LORD. Jesus Christ of Nazareth came, conceived by the Holy Spirit in and born of the virgin, Mary, espoused to Joseph (Matt. 1:18-25). He was born and raised a child of Israel, of the tribe of Judah, and He had brothers and sisters (Matt. 13:55, 56; Luke 2:41-52, Rev. 5:5). He began His earthly ministry at about the age of thirty, and for three and a half years; He healed, forgave, provided for and prophesied of things to come (Luke 3:23). And finally at Passover in 31 A.D.; He was crucified and died on the cross for the forgiveness of our sins, spilling His Holy and righteous blood. He was buried and the third day He arose to give us the hope and promise of eternal life in His Holy name. Alleluia and praise the LORD. Amen and Amen.

Land Sabbath

Leviticus 25:1-7 says, "And the LORD spake unto Moses in mount Sinai, saying, Speak unto the children of Israel, and say unto them, When ye come into the land which I give you, then shall the land keep a sabbath unto the LORD. Six years thou shalt sow thy field, and six years thou shalt prune thy vineyard, and gather in the fruit thereof; But in the seventh year shall be a sabbath of rest unto the land, a sabbath for the LORD: thou shalt neither sow thy field, nor prune thy vineyard. That which groweth of its own accord of thy harvest thou shalt not reap, neither gather the grapes of thy vine undressed: *for* it is a year of rest unto the land. And the sabbath of the land shall be meat for you; for thee, and for thy servant, and for thy maid, and for thy hired servant, and for thy stranger that sojourneth with thee. And for thy cattle, and for the beast that *are* in thy land, shall all the increase thereof be meat.".

Isaiah 40:22 says of God, "*It is* he that … stretcheth out the heavens as a curtain, and spreadeth them out as a tent to dwell in…". With this description, along with the idea's in appendix E of God clothing the heaven's with blackness, is it not then possible that beyond the veil of blackness in the outer expanse of the universe is a brightness that is of God, that goes on forever? Maybe this is what Jesus means, by us in Him and Him in us (John 14:20). And maybe that darkness is indeed a shade and a covering from God, the Father, Almighty, that covers us from His bright light, as He is a "… consuming fire…" (Deut. 4:24, Ps. 57:5, 11; 1 Tim. 6:16, Jam. 1:17). That being said, within the dark expanse of the universe, we also have God's creation; that is, the stars, sun, moon and our solar system in particular (Gen. 1:14-18). The Hubble telescope has found amongst other things, what some claim is images of galaxies being formed. And God says in Genesis, the stars are for a sign, along with the sun and moon; but we are not to worship the host of heaven (Gen. 1:14-18, Deut. 17:2-5). God says, He "… inhabiteth eternity…" (Isa. 57:15). So it is quite possible that God is giving us a glimpse, through these images, of His ability to increase and create, even a "…new heaven and a new earth…" (Isa. 65:17, 2 Pet. 3:13, Rev. 21:1). Isaiah 51:16 says of God, "…I may plant the heavens…". Psalm 147:4 says, "He telleth the number of the stars; he calleth them all by *their* names.". Jesus said His faithful followers names are written in heaven, God willing that is you and I, as well (Luke 10:17-20). Jeremiah 17:13 also speaks of our names being written in earth, this has everything to do with our resurrection, and the possibility of being like Adam and Eve, someday. Albeit in this verse, it seems to be because of punishment for not obeying God, not a blessing for obedience. Nevertheless, the book of Revelation of the New Testament speaks of us receiving a "…new name…", that no man knows, but those whom receive it (Rev. 2:17, 3:12). And both the New and Old Testament promise God and Jesus Christ of Nazareth's faithful followers a "…new heaven and a new earth…" with a "…new Jerusalem…" (Isa. 65:17, 66:22; 2 Pet. 3:13, Rev. 21:1, 2). Where the former things have passed away, neither do they come to mind, all tears will be wiped away, and there will be no more death, nor sorrow, no more crying, nor pain (Eccl. 1:11, Isa. 43:18, 51:11, 65:17; Jer. 31:12, John 16:22, Rev. 21:4). Alleluia and praise the LORD. Amen and Amen. Regarding our individuality in Jesus Christ of Nazareth's Holy name, the apostle, Paul, says, "*There is* one glory of the sun, and another glory of the moon, and another glory of the stars: for *one* star differeth from *another* star in glory." (1 Cor. 15:41). But there is a common salvation for all in Jesus Christ of Nazareth, whom died on the cross for the forgiveness of the sins of the whole world at Passover in 31 A.D., spilling His Holy and righteous blood. He was buried and He arose the third day to give us the hope and promise of eternal life in His Holy name. Alleluia and praise the LORD. Amen and Amen.

Obedience to God brings blessings and increase (Deut. 28:1-14). Of Abrahams seed, God says in Genesis 22:17, "That in blessing I will bless thee, and in multiplying I will multiply thy seed as the stars of the heaven, and as the sand which *is* upon the sea shore…". If we put these verses together with Jesus saying of Himself, "In my Father's house are many mansions: if *it were* not *so,* I would have told you. I go to prepare a place for you."; along with the prophecy of Jesus' government having an increase with no end, and the reality of God's work of "planting" the heavens (Isa. 9:7, 51:16; John 14:2). And Him encouraging us to, "Enlarge the place of thy tent, and let them stretch forth the curtains of thine habitations: spare not, lengthen thy cords, and strengthen thy stakes..." (Isa. 54:2). Then you may be able to see, that what God has planned for each man and woman here on earth, is much greater than just this life, it is life eternal and life more abundantly (John 10:10, 12:50). Alleluia and praise the LORD. Amen and Amen. But as Jesus said, "Which of you by taking thought can add one cubit unto his stature?" (Matt. 6:27). So the increase belongs to God, blessed be the LORD God, the Father, Almighty and blessed be His Holy name in Christ Jesus of Nazareth, His only begotten Son, with His Holy Spirit (Gen. 26:24, Deut. 15:14, Josh, 22:33, Judg. 5:9, 2 Sam. 22:47, 1 Ch. 29:14). Alleluia and praise the LORD. Jesus Christ of Nazareth died on the cross for the forgiveness of our sins at Passover in 31 A.D., spilling His Holy and righteous blood. He was buried and the third day He arose to give us the hope and promise of eternal life in His Holy name. Alleluia and praise the LORD. Amen and Amen. So ultimately we ought to pray "… Our Father which art in heaven, Hallowed be thy name. Thy kingdom come, Thy will be done in earth, as *it is* in heaven. …" (Matt. 6:9, 10). He asks us to love Him with all of our heart, mind, strength and soul, and love our neighbour as our self (Mark 12:33). We do this by following Jesus Christ of Nazareth and obeying God's commands in obedience to Him, through His Holy Spirit given to us, in the name of His only begotten Son, Jesus Christ of Nazareth. Jesus died on the cross for the forgiveness of our sins at Passover in 31 A.D., spilling His righteous and Holy blood. He was buried, and the third day He arose to give us the hope and promise of eternal life in His Holy name. Alleluia and praise the LORD. Amen and Amen. The moon is for a sign, and it is mostly desolate of inhabitants and formed things, at least as of the date of writing this book in 2019 A.D. (Gen. 1:14-18). This may be a very good example of what the earth was like, before God started the seven day creation week in the beginning (Gen. 1:2). And may be an example of what the earth will be like, even temporary in the future; as Jeremiah prophesied, "I beheld the earth, and, lo, *it was* without form, and void; and the heavens, and they *had* no light." (Jer. 4:23). God only knows for certain. To God be the glory in the truth of all of these things, in the name of His only begotten Son, Jesus Christ of Nazareth. Alleluia and praise the LORD. Amen and Amen.

Last Great Day

Daniel 7:9 says, "I beheld till the thrones were cast down, and the Ancient of days did sit, whose garment *was* white as snow, and the hoar of his head like the pure wool: his throne *was like* the fiery flame, *and* his wheels *as* burning fire." (Dan. 7:9). Jesus, during His transfiguration, was described as having His raiment, His garment, as white as snow (Mark 9:3). Jesus also said of Himself, "...Before Abraham was, I am." (John 8:58). This description of the Ancient of days is, no doubt, of Jesus Christ of Nazareth; as He said, "...All power is given unto me in heaven and in earth." (Matt. 28:18). Daniel 7:13 says, "I saw in the night visions, and, behold, *one* like the Son of man came with the clouds of heaven, and came to the Ancient of days, and they brought him near before him. And there was given him dominion, and glory, and a kingdom, that all people, nations, and languages, should serve him: his dominion *is* an everlasting dominion, which shall not pass away, and his kingdom *that* which shall not be destroyed.". This is a description again of Jesus Christ of Nazareth, inheriting everything from God, the Father, just as Jesus said during His earthly ministry in the early first century A.D. (Matt. 11:27, Luke 10:22, John 3:35, 13:3, 16:15, 17:10). He said, "I and *my* Father are one." (John 10:30). He calls us to be one in Him, even as He and His Father are one (John 17:22, 23). This is why the apostle, Paul, talks about followers of Christ as, the Church of God, and the body of Christ (1 Cor. 12:27). Alleluia and praise the LORD. Amen and Amen. Daniel 7:18 says, "But the saints of the most High shall take the kingdom, and possess the kingdom for ever, even for ever and ever.". Daniel 7:22 says, "Until the Ancient of days came, and judgement was given to the saints of the most High; and the time came that the saints possessed the kingdom.". And Daniel 7:27 says, "And the kingdom and dominion, and the greatness of the kingdom under the whole heaven, shall be given to the people of the saints of the most High, whose kingdom *is* an everlasting kingdom, and all dominions shall serve and obey him.". These few verses represent the authority God has given to us all; but ultimately, He still is sovereign over all things (John 1:1-3, Rev. 4:11). This is the freedom of choice He has given us from the beginning, with the choice of choosing the tree of life, or the tree of knowledge of good and evil (Gen. 2:9). It is the choice we have of obeying God, in His law and commands or doing it our own way (Deut. 30:19, 20). And ultimately, it is the choice we have to make, in whether or not we accept Jesus Christ of Nazareth as our LORD and Saviour, because He died on the cross for the forgiveness of our sins at Passover in 31 A.D., spilling His Holy and righteous blood. He was buried and He arose the third day to give us the hope and promise of eternal life in His Holy name. Alleluia and praise the LORD. Amen and Amen.

Revelation 20:11-15 says, "And I saw a great white throne, and him that sat on it, from whose face the earth and the heaven fled away; and there was found no place for them. And I saw the dead, small and great, stand before God; and the books were opened: and another book was opened, which is *the book* of life: and the dead were judged out of those things which were written in the books, according to their works. And the sea gave up the dead which were in it; and death and hell delivered up the dead which were in them: and they were judged every man according to their works. And death and hell were cast into the lake of fire. This is the second death. And whosoever was not found written in the book of life was cast into the lake of fire.". This is indeed the book of Revelation account of the Last Great Day, the final judgement, that the Holy Bible speaks of throughout, and Jesus Christ of Nazareth speaks of during His earthly ministry in the early first century A.D. (John 6:39, 40, 44, 54; 7:37, 11:1-37, 12:48). The books that are opened may be other religious texts, or accounts of our works, but ultimately the standard is the book of life, which is the Holy Bible of God, and our own life testimony in Christ Jesus of Nazareth's Holy name. As the Holy Bible says, "...there is none other name under heaven given among men, whereby we must be saved." (Acts 4:12). Alleluia and praise the LORD. Amen and Amen. This is echoed in Daniel 7:10, "A fiery stream issued and came forth from before him: thousand thousands ministered unto him, and ten thousand times ten thousand stood before him: the judgment was set, and the books were opened.". The thousand thousands are likely the one hundred and forty four thousand, elect, that is, saints, mentioned in the book of Revelation and throughout the Holy Bible, also referenced as angels coming with Christ at His return, to judge this world; included in the thousand thousands, would, I suppose, be the "...people of the saints...", those whom the saints directly influence in this life (Deut. 33:2, Ps. 68:17, Dan. 7:27, Matt. 13:37-43, 16:27, 25:31, Mark 8:38, Luke 9:26, Rev. 7, 14). And the ten thousand times ten thousand may represent the people whom the saints have responsibility to warn and teach, etc., more generally, in their life time; and likely represent all of the dead whom will be raised up and judged at the last day (Rev. 20:11-15). But ultimately we must remember that God is no respecter of persons (Acts 10:34). We all have the same reward in the end, as Jesus Christ of Nazareth gives all whom believe in Him eternal life (John 3:16). Alleluia and praise the LORD. Amen and Amen.

Revelation 3:21 says, "To him that overcometh will I grant to sit with me in my throne, even as I also overcame, and am set down with my Father in his throne.". Jesus showed us the truth of the resurrection in His own life, overcoming this world, before He even died on the cross for the forgiveness of our sins (John 16:33). But He did indeed take up His cross, dying on it, shedding His Holy and righteous blood for the forgiveness of our sins at Passover in 31 A.D.. Not only this, but He was buried, and He arose three days later to give us the hope and promise of eternal life in His Holy name. Alleluia and praise the LORD. He resurrected, at least, a few dead people during His earthly ministry, and spoke of the reality of our life being in the Spirit, not in the flesh (Matt. 9:18, 19, 23-26; Luke 7:11-17, John 6:63, 11:1-45). Jesus said to Martha, "And whosoever liveth and believeth in me shall never die. Believest thou this?" (John 11:26). Martha was the sister of Lazarus, whom was raised from the dead by Jesus after four days in the grave (John 11:1-45). This is the reality of the eternal life we have, in the life of Jesus Christ of Nazareth. He said of God, the Father, and Himself, "...this is life eternal, that they might know thee the only true God, and Jesus Christ, whom thou hast sent." (John 17:3). Alleluia and praise the LORD. Do you know Him, and His Father and ours? If not, what are you waiting for, repent and believe, ask Jesus Christ of Nazareth into your life, accepting His shed blood on the cross for the forgiveness of your sins at Passover in 31 A.D.. He died on the cross for the forgiveness of our sins, shedding His Holy and righteous blood. He was buried and He arose the third day for the hope and promise of eternal life in His Holy name. Alleluia and praise the LORD. Amen and Amen. Jesus ultimately used a parable of the labourers in the vineyard, to show that we all receive the same reward in the end, the man who labours from the early hours of the morning until evening, or the one whom labours only an hour at the end of the day, both received a penny for their efforts (Matt. 20:1-16). This may seem unjust, but the reality is, we are all sinners, and we all need forgiveness from God for our sins, no matter how "big" or "small", we or anyone else may think our sins are (Acts 10:34). This is why we all need Jesus Christ of Nazareth and His offering made on the cross for us, for the forgiveness of our sins at Passover in 31 A.D.. He died on the cross for the forgiveness of our sins, spilling His Holy and righteous blood, and He was buried. Not only this but He has given us life and life more abundantly, through His promises to us, confirmed in His resurrection after three days in the grave, for the hope and promise to all of eternal life in Jesus Christ of Nazareth's Holy name. Alleluia and praise the LORD. Amen and Amen.

Conclusion

Jesus said, "...The kingdom of God cometh not with observation: Neither shall they say, Lo here! or, lo there! for, behold, the kingdom of God is within you." (Luke 17:20, 21). God has a mind, and it is one, and He says the former things do not come to mind, neither are they remembered (Job 23:12, Eccl. 1:11, Isa. 43:18, 65:17; Rev. 21:4). This is a very good indication, that indeed, God plans to make all things new, in a "...new heaven and a new earth...", with the "...new Jerusalem..." (Rev. 21:1, 2, 5). That is, He plans to start from a clean slate, so to speak, when and if ever He decides to start anew with His creation, that is, all things that He has made, is making, and will make, visible and invisible (Col. 1:16, 17). Ezekiel speaks about us receiving a "...new heart..." and a "...new spirit..."; this is a good indication that we can indeed start a new life in the name of Jesus Christ of Nazareth, where our former thoughts, and deeds are no longer weighed in the balance of God's judgement (Ezek. 18:31, 36:26). This is the whole, entire and complete purpose of the cross of Jesus Christ of Nazareth. Alleluia and praise the LORD. Amen and Amen. He died on that cross at Passover in 31 A.D., so that we can be saved by His righteous and Holy blood spilt on the cross for the forgiveness of all of our sin. He was buried and the third day He arose to give us the hope and promise of eternal life in His Holy name. Alleluia and praise the LORD. Amen and Amen. Do you believe that Jesus Christ of Nazareth did all of this for you? If so, praise the LORD. Give Him thanks, and follow Him. Pray to Him for His Holy Spirit to dwell in you, to renew your mind, and give you a new purpose for your life here on earth, and in "the world to come", eternal life (Rom. 12:2). Alleluia and praise the LORD. Amen and Amen. John 1:1-5 says, "In the beginning was the Word, and the Word was with God, and the Word was God. The same was in the beginning with God. All things were made by him; and without him was not any thing made that was made. In him was life; and the life was the light of men. And the light shineth in darkness; and the darkness comprehended it not.". This means that God created you and I; and He does indeed have a good purpose for your existence, not only in this life, but God willing forever. Alleluia and praise the LORD. Amen and Amen.

Revelation 4:11 says, "Thou art worthy, O Lord, to receive glory and honour and power: for thou hast created all things, and for thy pleasure they are and were created.". Alleluia and praise the LORD. Amen and Amen. God said He was well pleased with His only begotten Son, Jesus Christ of Nazareth (Matt. 12:18). He made this clear on at least two separate occasions in the New Testament, the first was at Jesus' baptism by His earthly cousin, John, at about the age of thirty; and the second was at Jesus' transfiguration, witnessed by Peter, James and John, Jesus' disciples (Matt. 3:17, 17:5). So when we consider God's creation, and by what measure we ought to define God's pleasure, we need not look any further then Jesus Christ of Nazareth, and His works. Alleluia and praise the LORD. Amen and Amen. The parable of the ten virgins in the gospel according to Matthew and the "…new Jerusalem…" coming down from heaven spoken of in the book of Revelation may be good indicators of God's ultimate plan for this world, and the whole universe in general (Matt. 25:1-12, Rev. 21:2). The parable is such that five virgins keep their lamps full of oil. That is in reference to the Holy Spirit and the knowledge of the truth in Christ Jesus of Nazareth, and the other five do not, and are encouraged to go buy oil. But when the five went to buy the oil, the wedding supper started and only the five with their lamps ready and full were let in (Matt. 25:1-12). Some may say, well this parable supports polygamy, but I do not think so at all; actually when we reference this with the "…new Jerusalem…", which is the bride, that comes down from heaven, adorned for her husband, and the tabernacle of God is with men, that is "men" plural, then we can see that the wedding supper is not necessarily for one "couple" (Rev. 21:2, 3). There are likely multiples of the bride and bridegroom, multiple new earths, worlds; with similar Adam and Eve like beginnings to come in each, possibly expanding the universe forever, God knows (Heb. 1:2, 11:3). These two similitudes of the wedding supper, may be one of the main keys for describing God's eternal plan of expanding, that is, growing His kingdom, through His Holy Spirit, in the name of His only begotten Son, Jesus Christ of Nazareth (John 14:2). Alleluia and praise the LORD. As it says in Isaiah, "Of the increase of *his* government and peace *there shall be* no end..." (Isa. 9:7). And we can all partake in the plan of God by accepting, God, the Father, and His only begotten Son, Jesus Christ of Nazareth with His Holy Spirit, into our life. This is done by repenting, accepting that we are sinners; unrighteous in and of ourselves, broken, and need a Saviour. And Jesus Christ of Nazareth is that Saviour, He died on the cross for the forgiveness of our sins at Passover in 31 A.D., He was buried and on the third day He arose, giving us all the hope and promise of eternal life in His Holy name. Alleluia and praise the LORD. Amen and Amen.

Jesus' crucifixion, burial and resurrection week timeline

Sunday

Jesus entry into Jerusalem on donkey's colt, as King of Israel (Matt. 21:1-16)

Sunday Evening — Monday

Woman anoints Jesus' head Monday Evening with "very precious ointment" (Matt. 26:7) Other events of Monday of crucifixion week (Matt. 21:17-46; Matt. 22-26:1-16)

Tuesday

Passover meal eaten with disciples Tuesday evening (Matt. 26:18-30) Passover starts at evening before day of crucifixion (Gen. 1:5, Lev. 23:5)

Tuesday Evening — Wednesday

Passover day (John 18:39) Jesus crucified (Mark 15:34) Jesus body given to Joseph of Arimathea (John 19:38-40) Jesus buried (John 19:41, 42)

Wednesday Evening — Thursday

High day (John 19:31) Holy day (Lev. 23:6-11; Matt. 21:1-11) First day of Unleavened bread (Lev. 23:6)

Thursday Evening — Friday

Women bought spices (Mark 16:1, Luke 23:56)

Friday Evening — Saturday

Jesus likely resurrected on the third day, Saturday afternoon (Gen. 1:5, Matt. 12:39, 40)

Saturday Evening — Sunday

Women visit tomb (Luke 24:1) Jesus reveals Himself to Mary Magdalene (John 20:11-17) Jesus reveals Himself to disciples (John 20:19)

Note: This would fulfill very well the prophecy of Daniel about the Messiah, Jesus Christ of Nazareth, being cut off in the middle of the week literally. He came into Jerusalem riding on an asses colt, with the multitudes worshipping Him (Dan. 9:26, 27; Matt. 21:1-11). And in a few days, on Wednesday, precisely in the middle of the week, He was betrayed and crucified. Jesus died on the cross for the forgiveness of our sins at Passover in 31 A.D., shedding His Holy and righteous blood. He was buried and the third day He arose, overcoming death and sin, to show us the hope and promise of eternal life we all have in His Holy name. Alleluia and praise the LORD. Amen and Amen.

The other fulfillment of this, is regarding Jesus Christ of Nazareth being cutoff in the midst of His ministry, three and a half years in. The "great tribulation" likely being the second half of this prophetic fulfillment of the final week of Daniel's seventy week prophecy, using the "day for a year" principle (Ezek. 4:6, Dan. 9:24-27). I have written other books on this subject in greater detail and have mentioned the subject briefly in this book. But place your trust in God and His Holy Word the Holy Bible through the inspiration of the Holy Spirit, in Christ Jesus of Nazareth first and foremost!! Alleluia and praise the LORD. Amen and Amen.

APPENDIX E

Church, Feast of Tabernacles, Messianic Age and the "World to Come"

Introduction

2 Peter 1:10 and 11 say, "Wherefore the rather, brethren, give diligence to make your calling and election sure: for if ye do these things, ye shall never fall: For so an entrance shall be ministered unto you abundantly into the everlasting kingdom of our Lord and Saviour Jesus Christ.". In the Old Testament, when the priests were charged with the repairing of the first temple in Jehoash and Josiah's time, as kings over Judah; it is mentioned, the priests faithfully gave the money to those whom would pay the workmen, and whom would do the work, respectively (2 Kings 12:15, 22:7). Workers are also mentioned to have done their job faithfully, in restoring the first temple, during Josiah's reign (2 Chr. 34:12). The apostle, Paul, says in 1 Corinthians 4:1 and 2, "Let a man so account of us, as of the ministers of Christ, and stewards of the mysteries of God. Moreover it is required in stewards, that a man be found faithful.". Similar examples are seen when the Israelites of the tribe of Judah, were sent back to Jerusalem, from captivity in Babylon, to build the second temple; the appointed ruler of Jerusalem, Hananiah, was said to be faithful (Neh. 7:2). The treasurers, priest and scribe were also said to have been faithful (Neh. 13:13). These may be perfect examples in how we ought to be "building" the kingdom of God; that is, through faith, which is a gift from God, by grace (Eph. 2:8, 9). And we must remember that ultimately; Jesus Christ of Nazareth, God, the Father, and the Holy Spirit are Faithful and True (Rev. 3:14, 19:11). And Jesus Christ of Nazareth is the author and finisher of our faith (Heb. 12:2). There is a parable, Jesus uses, of the growth of the kingdom of God; and it is regarding a sower, whom plants a seed and does not know how it grows up (Mark 4:26-30). This is another example of God's kingdom and how it has, is and will continue to grow here on earth, and in the "world to come", eternal life (Mark 10:30). Alleluia and praise the LORD. Jesus did indeed say He would come as a thief, so we ought to watch and pray (Matt. 24:42-44). Nevertheless, the remainder of this appendix is about God's kingdom in this physical world, through fellowship at Church, in the world through work, in things to come, in the "Messianic Age" and the "...new heaven and a new earth...", the "world to come" (Acts 2:42, 2 Tim. 3:17, Rev. 5:10, 20:4, 21:1, 22:1-5). So read on to learn more about these subjects. To God be the glory in the truth of all of these things. Alleluia and praise the LORD. Amen and Amen.

Church and business

Ezekiel chapter ten can likely be interpreted in many ways, but one interpretation I have found, was that of a church service. It starts with, "Then I looked, and, behold, in the firmament that was above the head of the cherubims there appeared over them as it were a sapphire stone, as the appearance of the likeness of a throne." (Ezek. 10:1). In Churches, typically traditional ones, there are stained glass windows, and they usually depict Biblical scenes. Often at the front of the Church, is the memorial of Jesus Christ of Nazareth in stained glass, depicted in one form or another. This would describe the

"…likeness of a throne…"; the cherubims being the ministers below, ministering to the congregation. Ezekiel 10:2 continues, "And he spake unto the man clothed with linen, and said, Go in between the wheels, *even* under the cherub, and fill thine hand with coals of fire from between the cherubims, and scatter *them* over the city. And he went in in my sight.". The person clothed with linen is the individual person whom attends the Church service, and the "…coals of fire…" may represent the "Word of God", the sermons, readings, songs spoken of and sang by the ministers during the service, that are all to be obeyed and done after leaving the church service. Ezekiel 10:3 says, "Now the cherubims stood on the right side of the house, when the man went in; and the cloud filled the inner court.". This describes the "preacher" at the "pulpit", the congregation coming in, and the presence of God in the cloud. Ezekiel 10:4 says, "Then the glory of the LORD went up from the cherub, *and stood* over the threshold of the house; and the house was filled with the cloud, and the court was full of the brightness of the LORD's glory.". This can describe the praising of God by the congregation, the offerings, and communion, the taking of the bread and wine in remembrance that Christ died on the cross for the forgiveness of our sins, shedding His Holy and righteous blood at Passover in 31 A.D.. He was buried and He arose the third day for our hope and promise of eternal life in His Holy name. Alleluia and praise the LORD. Amen and Amen.

Ezekiel 10:5 says, "And the sound of the cherubims' wings was heard *even* to the outer court, as the voice of the Almighty God when he speaketh.". Ministers often wear a robe that drape over the length of the arm and appear like a cape or wings. This "voice" could also be associated with the bells, organ music and singing of the congregation, in general. As the Holy Bible of God says, God inhabits our praise (Ps. 22:3). Ezekiel 10:6 says, "And it came to pass, *that* when he had commanded the man clothed with linen, saying, Take fire from between the wheels, from between the cherubims; then he went in, and stood beside the wheels.". This can be in reference to listening to the readings, sermon, communion and songs of praise to God Almighty. Alleluia and praise the LORD. Ezekiel 10:7 says, "And *one* cherub stretched forth his hand from between the cherubims unto the fire that *was* between the cherubims, and took *thereof,* and put *it* into the hands of *him that was* clothed with linen: who took *it,* and went out.". This describes the blessings given at the end of the service. Ezekiel 10:8 says, "And there appeared in the cherubims the form of a man's hand under their wings.". This is the first clear indicator that the cherubims are people. Ezekiel 10:9 says, "And when I looked, behold the four wheels by the cherubims, one wheel by one cherub, and another wheel by another cherub: and the appearance of the wheels *was* as the colour of a beryl stone.". This would describe the congregation on either side of the isle way of the Church. They appear as wheels when they go up for communion and come back to their seats; the four wheels could be two on each side, one representing the husband and one the wife on each side. Ezekiel 10:10 says, "And *as for* their appearances, they four had one likeness, as if a wheel had been in the midst of a wheel.". This describes the congregation and the minister, but also the wife and husband; and ultimately, the Church and God, the Father, in Christ Jesus of Nazareth, through His Holy Spirit in us, and around us, and us in Him (John 6:56). Alleluia and praise the LORD. Amen and Amen.

Ezekiel 10:11 says, "When they went, they went upon their four sides; they turned not as they went, but to the place whither the head looked they followed it; they turned not as they went.". Jesus Christ of Nazareth, through the Holy Spirit, is the head of the Church (1 Cor. 11:3). Of course, naturally, our physical head usually faces in the direction that we as individuals travel; and in the church service, this can describe the communion; standing, walking to the altar, kneeling, walking back to the seat, etc..

Alleluia and praise the LORD. Ezekiel 10:12 says, "And their whole body, and their backs, and their hands, and their wings, and the wheels, *were* full of eyes round about, *even* the wheels that they four had.". This certainly describes the eyes of the body of the congregation and ministers, even extending to those they have relationships with outside of the physical building of the church. As Jesus Christ of Nazareth said, there will come a time and now is, where we will not worship God in Jerusalem or in Samaria, but in spirit and in truth (John 4:21-23). Ezekiel 10:13 says, "As for the wheels, it was cried unto them in my hearing, O wheel.". This shows the spiritual oneness of the Church of God, that Jesus Christ of Nazareth describes in the New Testament (John 17:22, 23). Ezekiel 10:14 says, "And every one had four faces: the first face *was* the face of a cherub, and the second face *was* the face of a man, and the third the face of a lion, and the fourth the face of an eagle.". These four faces describe the attributes of the people, the face of a cherub representing godliness, the face of a man representing mankind, the face of a lion representing dominion and the face of an eagle representing freedom of choice and freedom, in general. Alleluia and praise the Lord. Amen and Amen.

Ezekiel 10:15 says, "And the cherubims were lifted up. This *is* the living creature that I saw by the river of Chebar.". This describes the conclusion of the service, with the exit of the ministers and congregation. Ezekiel 10:16 says, "And when the cherubims went, the wheels went by them: and when the cherubims lifted up their wings to mount up from the earth, the same wheels also turned not from beside them.". Again, this suggests unity of the ministers and congregations, in the Holy Spirit of God, even after leaving the physical church building. Ezekiel 10:17 says, "When they stood, *these* stood; and when they were lifted up, *these* lifted up themselves *also:* for the spirit of the living creature *was* in them.". This is another confirmation of unity in the body of Christ, as Paul, the apostle, also speaks about in one of his epistles (Rom. 12:4, 5). Ezekiel 10:18 says, "Then the glory of the LORD departed from off the threshold of the house, and stood over the cherubims.". This could describe the change in position of the congregants and the ministers; that is, moving from place to place during the service and after the service is complete. Ezekiel 10:19 says, "And the cherubims lifted up their wings, and mounted up from the earth in my sight: when they went out, the wheels also *were* beside them, and *every one* stood at the door of the east gate of the LORD's house; and the glory of the God of Israel *was* over them above.". This can describe the exiting from the physical church building, with God's Holy Spirit coming with us, when we go into the world (Mark 16:15). Ezekiel 10:20 says, "This *is* the living creature that I saw under the God of Israel by the river of Chebar; and I knew that they *were* the cherubims.". The living creature, in general, is mankind; our family life, work life and spiritual life, as I interpreted in an appendix in another book I wrote, "Heaven, Hell and the Resurrection", using Ezekiel chapter one for interpretation. Ezekiel 10:21 says, "Every one had four faces apiece, and every one four wings; and the likeness of the hands of a man *was* under their wings.". This again, is a sign of the nature in mankind; the godlikeness, through God, the Father's, Holy Spirit, in Christ Jesus of Nazareth's Holy name, and our natural human nature, self-governance and freedom. Alleluia and praise the LORD. Amen and Amen. Last, Ezekiel 10:22 says, "And the likeness of their faces *was* the same faces which I saw by the river of Chebar, their appearances and themselves: they went every one straight forward.". Jesus says in the New Testament that the strait gate and narrow way leads to life (Matt. 7:14). Alleluia and praise the LORD. Amen and Amen.

Business; I have heard there is a five year timeline for a business to succeed or fail, as a business concept teaching. We may be able to see a business model, in the planting and growth of a fruit bearing tree; that is, plant its seed, let it grow for three years and the firstfruits are left alone (Lev. 19:23). In business, this could be considered capital, used to pay employees, savings, etc.. The fourth year's fruit is for God (Lev. 19:24). In business, this may be considered for outreach and partnership with a charity group or the like, etc.. And the fifth year's fruit can be eaten (Lev. 19:25). In business, this maybe a year to "pay yourself", if you are a business owner, etc.. The sixth year is the same as the fifth, and maybe used to sell, and/or store seed for growth of crop, etc. (Lev. 25:3, 20-22). In business, this would be a time for expansion, and preparation for other investments and plans to stabilize and possibly grow the business. The seventh year is used to give rest to the land; that is, the crops are left to grow and be gleaned as needed (Lev. 25:4-7). This is self-explanatory, but basically we all need rest, and the seventh year should be for such; also it may be a good year to consider the charitable partnership of the business, whatever that may be. According to the Holy Bible of God, leasing and usury are not looked upon positively by God (Ps. 4:2, 5:6; Ezek. 18:10-13). That being said, there are some Old Testament laws, regarding usury and lending, including the release of bondservants, if the servant desires, in the seventh year (Lev. 25:36, 37; Deut. 15:12-14, 23:19, 20; Prov. 28:8). And we are not to lend unto our brothers with usury (Ex. 22:25). But our reality is in Jesus Christ of Nazareth. Alleluia and praise the LORD. Amen and Amen. Jesus gave a parable of the growing tree. If it does not bear fruit the third year, He says to tend it for a fourth year (Luke 13:6-9). In general, this is a sign to give life a chance. Also, Jesus cursed a fig tree for not bearing fruit (Matt. 21:19). So ultimately, just like our life, in general; all of these things are in the hands of the Almighty God, the Father, in Christ Jesus of Nazareth's Holy name, through His Holy Spirit. Alleluia and praise the LORD. Amen and Amen.

Feast of Tabernacles and Messianic Age

Revelation 21:24 and 26 say, "And the nations of them which are saved shall walk in the light of it: and the kings of the earth do bring their glory and honour into it. ... And they shall bring the glory and honour of the nations into it.". These verses are referencing the "...new Jerusalem..." in the book of Revelation, which is spiritual first and foremost and is part of the "...new heaven and a new earth...", discussed further at the end of this section and in the next, but this verse is also relevant to the "Messianic Age" (Rev. 21:1, 2). In the light of the "Messianic Age", it will likely reflect the responsibility of the heads of state and their families, "...glory and honour..." of the nations, to attend the feast of Tabernacles in the "Messianic age", in Jerusalem, in the newly built temple according to Ezekiel's vision (Ezek. 40-47, Zech. 14:16, 17). God is our glory and is glorified by His presence in us, through His Holy Spirit, in Jesus Christ of Nazareth's Holy name (Ps. 3:3, John 17:10). And it is only by God's Holy Spirit, by the blood of the Lamb, Jesus Christ of Nazareth that we can obey and honour Him. It is by the glory of His only begotten Son, Jesus Christ of Nazareth, that we can be glorified or that we can glorify God. Jesus died on the cross for the forgiveness of our sins at Passover in 31 A.D., shedding His Holy and righteous blood. He was buried and arose the third day for our hope and promise of eternal life in His Holy name. Alleluia and praise the LORD. Amen and Amen. It is only by the blood of the Lamb, by His offering on the cross for the forgiveness of our sins, that we can enter into the city of God. That is, no abominable thing can enter into it (Rev. 21:27). We must be cleansed of our sins in order to enter into God's eternal kingdom; and this cleansing is a gift, paid by the blood of Jesus Christ of Nazareth on the cross. It is free for us to receive, by grace through faith, that is also a gift (Eph. 2:8, 9). Alleluia and praise the LORD. Amen and Amen. This had its foreshadowing at Passover, during the Exodus from Egypt, by the Israelites, around 1518 B.C., whom applied the blood of the Passover lamb to their house door posts and lintel (Ex. 12:21-24). So the destroyer would not come into their house and destroy their first born (Ex. 12:23). Alleluia and praise the LORD. Amen and Amen. Jesus kept this same Passover, and made the new covenant clear to us, by the shedding of His own blood on the cross for the forgiveness of our sins and the gift of eternal life in His Holy name, instituting the eating of unleavened bread and the drinking of wine at Passover, as a sign in remembrance of His sacrifice for us all at Passover in 31 A.D. (Matt. 26:17-28). He died on the cross at Passover in 31 A.D.. He was buried and the third day He arose to give us the hope and promise of eternal life in His Holy name. Alleluia and praise the LORD. Amen and Amen.

The Land; Isaiah 8:7 and 8 say, "Now therefore, behold, the Lord bringeth up upon them the waters of the river, strong and many, *even* the king of Assyria, and all his glory: and he shall come up over all his channels, and go over all his banks: And he shall pass through Judah; he shall overflow and go over, he shall reach *even* to the neck; and the stretching out of his wings shall fill the breadth of thy land, O Immanuel.". Isaiah 8:10 says, "Take counsel together, and it shall come to nought; speak the word, and it shall not stand: for God *is* with us.". Immanuel means "God with us", and this was the name given to Jesus Christ of Nazareth; in Old Testament prophecy, and mentioned in the New Testament account of His birth (Isa. 7:14, Matt. 1:23). This prophecy in Isaiah, speaks of Jesus overcoming the world, but also, king Herod's failure to kill Jesus, after Jesus' birth (Matt. 2:13-21, John 16:33). Isaiah 62:4 says, "Thou shalt no more be termed Forsaken; neither shall thy land any more be termed Desolate: but thou shalt be called Hephzibah, and thy land Beulah: for the LORD delighteth in thee, and thy land shall be married.". Of course, we are from the dust, and are dust; so our bodies are literally a part of the land, as our first father was created from it physically (Gen. 1:26, Isa. 43:27). But in Jesus Christ of Nazareth, we are born both of water, the natural, and the spirit, the heavenly (John 1:12, 13; 3:5-8). Alleluia and praise the LORD. Amen and Amen. After the flood, Genesis 8:20-22 say, "And Noah builded an altar unto the LORD; and took of every clean beast, and of every clean fowl, and offered burnt offerings on the altar. And the LORD smelled a sweet savour; and the LORD said in his heart, I will not again curse the ground any more for man's sake; for the imagination of man's heart is evil from his youth; neither will I again smite any more every thing living, as I have done. While the earth remaineth, seedtime and harvest, and cold and heat, and summer and winter, and day and night shall not cease.". The curse for disobedience to God's command to keep the feast in the "Messianic Age" is spoken of in Zechariah 14:16-19; it says, "And it shall come to pass, *that* every one that is left of all the nations which came against Jerusalem shall even go up from year to year to worship the King, the LORD of hosts, and to keep the feast of tabernacles. And it shall be, *that* whoso will not come up of *all* the families of the earth unto Jerusalem to worship the King, the LORD of hosts, even upon them shall be no rain. And if the family of Egypt go not up, and come not, that *have* no *rain;* there shall be the plague, wherewith the LORD will smite the heathen that come not up to keep the feast of tabernacles. This shall be the punishment of Egypt, and the punishment of all nations that come not up to keep the feast of tabernacles.". Nevertheless, regardless of the truth of all of these things, our reality is in Jesus Christ of Nazareth, whom died on the cross for the forgiveness of our sins at Passover in 31 A.D., shedding His Holy and righteous blood. He was buried and the third day He arose to give us the hope and promise of eternal life in His Holy name. Alleluia and praise the LORD. Amen and Amen.

The "Messianic Age" and the "New Jerusalem"; Ezekiel 47:12 says, "And by the river upon the bank thereof, on this side and on that side, shall grow all trees for meat, whose leaf shall not fade, neither shall the fruit thereof be consumed: it shall bring forth new fruit according to his months, because their waters they issued out of the sanctuary: and the fruit thereof shall be for meat, and the leaf thereof for medicine.". Revelation 22:2 says, "In the midst of the street of it, and on either side of the river, *was there* the tree of life, which bare twelve *manner of* fruits, *and* yielded her fruit every month: and the leaves of the tree *were* for the healing of the nations.". This may represent the tree of life inscribed on the temple buildings, a palm tree, with two cherubs on either side of it (Ez. 41:18). It is also a sign of the husband and wife being fruitful and multiplying; as will be spoken of in greater detail in the next section (Gen. 1:26-28). The leaves may represent what covers us; our words, our hair, clothing, etc.; genealogy, family tree, etc., and ultimately, God Almighty (Ps. 17:8, 9). This may also be a sign of Adam and Eve; with the fig leaves sewn together for aprons, which covered their nakedness (Gen. 3:7). Also, the twelve tribes of Israel will be on either side of the temple in their lands allotted to them according to Ezekiel 48. These will be the twelve fruits, descendants of the twelve tribes of Israel living in Israel proper, as part of that tree of life (Rev. 22:2). Of course, this has been taking place already, but to my knowledge of the most recent political and geographic boundaries, the Ezekiel 48 land allotments have yet to be completely sorted out, God willing, as of the date of writing this book in 2019 A.D.. Ultimately, Jesus Christ of Nazareth and God, the Father, through His Holy Spirit; are the root of the tree of life, the water of the river of life, and the temple of God (Rev. 22:1-4). That is, it is God's Holy Spirit, whom is also with us, and in us, whom everything comes from; as we receive, God, the Father's, only begotten Son, Jesus Christ of Nazareth as our Lord and Saviour. Alleluia and praise the LORD. Amen and Amen.

World to come

Jesus said a scribe instructed unto the Kingdom of heaven brings forth both the old and the new (Matt. 13:52). So let us now talk about the creation in the beginning and the Garden of Eden (Gen. 1-2:3). Genesis 1:1 and 2 say, "In the beginning God created the heaven and the earth. And the earth was without form, and void; and darkness *was* upon the face of the deep. And the spirit of God moved upon the face of the waters.". Before God made the light there was darkness, and as mentioned in the Holy Bible, in other books I have written and even in other appendices in this book; it would seem that God is going to turn out the lights so to speak on this universe for some amount of time before the creation of the new heaven and a new earth (Jer. 4:23). But we need not worry about this; as God's kingdom is a spiritual one, first and foremost (John 4:24). God is a spirit after all, and we are to worship Him in spirit and in truth (John 4:24). Psalm 139:12 says, "Yea, the darkness hideth not from thee; but the night shineth as the day: the darkness and the light *are* both alike *to thee*.". Isaiah 50:3 says, "I clothe the heavens with blackness, and I make sackcloth their covering.". And Jeremiah outright says of God, "…I am black…" (Jer. 8:21). A psalmist compares his life to a shadow; he says "My days *are* like a shadow that declineth…" (Ps. 102:11). And the feast days, spoken of in the Holy Bible of God, and mentioned throughout this book, are said to be a shadow of good things to come (Col. 2:16, 17; Heb. 10:1). My point in all of this is, that God is even in the darkest of dark places (Ps. 112:4, John 1:5). He created them! Alleluia and praise the LORD. As King David said of God, "If I ascend up into heaven, thou *art* there: if I make my bed in hell, behold, thou *art there*." (Ps. 139:8). And ultimately, we have our hope in Jesus Christ of Nazareth; whom tasted death for all of us, so that we do not need to (John 11:26, Heb. 2:9). And just like God is in the darkness, He is also the light, as John describes Him in Jesus Christ of Nazareth and as Jesus Christ reveals Himself during the transfiguration, speaking with Moses and Elijah (Matt. 17:2, 3; John 1:4,5, 7; 8:12). His face is described as shining like the sun, and His garments shining as white as light (Matt. 17:2). Alleluia and praise the LORD. Amen and Amen.

Revelation 21:1-5 says, "And I saw a new heaven and a new earth: for the first heaven and the first earth were passed away; and there was no more sea. And I John saw the holy city, new Jerusalem, coming down from God out of heaven, prepared as a bride adorned for her husband. And I heard a great voice out of heaven saying, Behold, the tabernacle of God *is* with men, and he will dwell with them, and they shall be his people, and God himself shall be with them, *and be* their God. And God shall wipe away all tears from their eyes; and there shall be no more death, neither sorrow, nor crying, neither shall there be any more pain: for the former things are passed away. And he that sat upon the throne said, Behold, I make all things new. And he said unto me, Write: for these words are true and faithful.". I spoke about this subject in greater detail in my book, "Heaven, Hell and the Resurrection", but the Holy Bible of God does a fine job of describing it (Rev. 21, 22). Jesus said in John 14:2, "In my Father's house are many mansions: if *it were* not *so,* I would have told you. I go to prepare a place for you.". Isaiah said of Jesus, God, the Father, and the Holy Spirit, "Of the increase of *his* government and peace *there shall be* no end...." (Isa. 9:7). Could this not be describing the growth of God's family into the unknown parts of the Universe, possibly creating new solar systems, worlds, to inhabit, etc.? Isaiah 52:2 says, "Shake thyself from the dust; arise, *and* sit down, O Jerusalem: loose thyself from the bands of thy neck, O captive daughter of Zion.". Does this not sound like Adam being formed from the dust in the beginning??? God only knows for certain, what He has planned for mankind; but for us, we need not worry, as mentioned, Jesus is preparing our habitation, not only in the world to come, but for our life here on earth today, tomorrow and forever more in His Holy name. Alleluia and praise the LORD. Amen and Amen.

Garden of Eden like; The Tree of Life is possibly a date palm tree or olive tree. There is a palm tree used in the artistry of the temple of Ezekiel's vision, as mentioned in the previous section (Ezek. 40:16, 22, 26, 31, 34, 37; 41:18-20, 25, 26). And in the book of Revelation, two trees are on either side of the river, giving twelve manner of fruit, as mentioned in the previous section (Rev. 22:2). As I have mentioned in another book, this likely represents the monthly potential for a husband and wife to produce the fruit of conception; that is, child bearing. This is also the similitude of Jesus Christ of Nazareth and the Church of God, the body of Christ; and the marriage relationship, in general, between husband and wife, two becoming one flesh, in a holy and sanctified marriage of God (Gen. 2:24, Heb. 13:4, Rev. 19:7-9). This all being said; the olive tree may very well be the best candidate for the tree of life, if it was a literal natural tree in the Garden of Eden. The olive is used practically and produces fruit. It was the leaf from the olive tree that was found by the dove sent from the ark after the flood (Gen. 8:11). Olive oil was, and is used as fuel in the lamps, in the meat offerings mentioned in the Old Testament, and to anoint people for various reasons (Ex. 27:20; 29:39-41; 30:24, 25). The tree of knowledge of good and evil may very well have been the fig tree (Gen. 2:9). Jesus cursed a fig tree (Matt. 21:19). Ezekiel describes a tree with leaves that are for medicine (Ezek. 47:12). And Adam and Eve sowed fig leaves together to cover themselves, after their eyes were opened to their nakedness, because of eating from the tree of knowledge of good and evil (Gen. 3:7). Jeremiah spoke of evil figs and good figs (Jer. 24). King Hezekiah was healed of a deadly disease after; repenting, praying and rubbing figs on his inflammation (Isa. 38:21). Generally, figs are sweet. Even if the fruit of the tree was not unhealthy in a physical sense, God said not to eat it, but Adam and Eve ate it anyway (Gen. 2:16, 17; 3:6). That was the true breaking of God's command, the spiritual covenant God made with Adam and Eve (Gen. 2:16, 17). Of course, traditionally, the tree of knowledge of good and evil is suggested to be an apple tree; but I would suggest the Holy Bible of God shows little, if any, evidence of this being the truth. This all being said, we must also remember that the tree of knowledge of good and evil, had good in it. And Jesus admonishes us to either make the whole tree good or evil (Matt. 12:33). So it is ultimately our choice what we do with the knowledge of good and evil. Do we choose the good and eschew the evil or do we give into temptation? This is the freedom God has given us, and in His only begotten Son, Jesus Christ of Nazareth, He has overcome all of the evil of this world and any other and has made it subject unto Him (John 16:33). Alleluia and praise the LORD. Amen and Amen.

Conclusion

Attending church and faith; Romans10:14 and 15 say, "How then shall they call on him in whom they have not believed? and how shall they believe in him of whom they have not heard? and how shall they hear without a preacher? And how shall they preach, except they be sent? as it is written, How beautiful are the feet of them that preach the gospel of peace, and bring glad tidings of good things!". Romans 10:17 says, "So then faith *cometh* by hearing, and hearing by the word of God.". Overcoming evil with good, God is good (Ps. 144:2, Rom. 12:21). With regards to the feast of Tabernacles; it is interesting that in Matthew 5:44 and 45, it says, "But I say unto you, Love your enemies, bless them that curse you, do good to them that hate you, and pray for them which despitefully use you, and persecute you; That ye may be the children of your Father which is in heaven: for he maketh his sun to rise on the evil and on the good, and sendeth rain on the just and on the unjust.". My point is, regarding the rain being held back from the countries whom do not go to Jerusalem for the feast of Tabernacles (Zech. 14:16-19). It would truly be a miracle if the Zechariah commandment was fulfilled, and in order to not make God, nor Jesus a liar, I would suggest then that both Zechariah's prophecy and Jesus' words will be fulfilled together. Time will tell what will be, but of course Jesus has been given all power in earth and in heaven, so no doubt, He can make all things possible (Matt. 19:26, 28:18). Jesus said, "…a kingdom…divided against itself…cannot stand. …Satan…hath an end." (Mark 3:24-26, Eph. 4:27). Jesus said, He is building His church and the gates of hell shall not prevail against it (Matt. 16:18). Alleluia and praise the LORD. Amen and Amen. Jesus said the kingdom of God does not come by observation, but it is within us (Luke 17:20, 21). As we have received Christ; the first time, our first Love, we have been saved from that day forward (1 John 4:19, Rev. 2:4). Alleluia and praise the LORD. He asks us to strengthen ourselves in the things that we have learned of Him (Rev. 3:2). He calls us to keep our lamp filled with oil (Matt. 25:1-13). These are all admonishments to continue in the faith of Christ Jesus of Nazareth, as our Lord and Saviour, until the "end", whenever and however that comes about (Matt. 10:22). This is our daily task in this world, and in the "world to come"; to take up our cross daily and follow Jesus Christ of Nazareth, as there is no other name under heaven whereby we can be saved (Luke 9:23, Acts. 4:12). Jesus Christ of Nazareth died on the cross for the forgiveness of our sins at Passover in 31 A.D., shedding His Holy and righteous blood. He was buried and the third day He arose to give us the hope and promise of eternal life in His Holy name. Alleluia and praise the LORD. Amen and Amen.

APPENDIX F

References

Books

1. The fall feasts of Israel, by Mitch and Zhava Glaser, 1987, Moody Press Chicago

Websites

1. Chabad.org
2. Skyviewcafe.com
3. https://www.ccel.org/ccel/josephus/complete.toc.html, retrieved 08/01/2018
4. http://www.cgsf.org/dbeattie/calendar, retrieved 31/12/2017
5. http://www.bethlehemstar.com/starry-dance/westward-leading/, retrieved 25/08/2017

Other

1. Joe Amaral suggested Jesus born on 1 Tishri, 1st day of 7th month of Hebrew Calendar, 100 Huntley street interview March 2015; email confirmation suggested 3 B.C. as year of birth - https://www.youtube.com/watch?v=B5Pjh0eVEik, retrieved 31/12/2017
2. John Reid suggests approximate time of Jesus birth to be between September 16 and 29, 4 B.C. http://www.sabbath.org/index.cfm/fuseaction/Library.sr/CT/ARTB/k/568/When-Was-Jesus-Born.htm, retrieved 03/01/2018
3. Barry Carter's astronomical analysis suggests Jupiter, Venus and Regulus conjunction on August 17, 2 B.C.; placing the wise men's visitation to the young child Jesus in late 2 B.C. (Matt. 2:1-12) - https://astronomy.stackexchange.com/questions/11456/has-the-conjunction-between-venus-jupiter-and-regulus-only-occurred-twice-in-2, retrieved 03/01/2018
4. Jupiter (King planet), Venus (Morningstar), Regulus (Lions heart) in constellation of Leo - https://mygodandyoursjesuschrist.com/2015/06/28/the-messiahs-star-jupitervenus-conjunction-and-the-second-coming-of-jesus/, retrieved 03/01/2018
5. This reference suggests the magi may have visited Jesus as a young child December 25th in 2 B.C. - http://www.bethlehemstar.com/starry-dance/to-stop-a-star/, retrieved 25/08/2017
6. Search for the constellation of Virgo on google - https://www.google.ca/search?q=virgo&client=firefox-b&dcr=0&source=lnms&tbm=isch&sa=X&ved=0ahUKEwjZo6DAmcvYAhUQ6mMKHWijB28Q_AUICigB&biw=1366&bih=635, retrieved 09/01/2018

Note: The author does not guarantee the availability of all references, especially websites, as organizations from time to time change names, addresses and discontinue services. Nor does the author guarantee the accuracy of the references. As the Bible says, "Prove all things; hold fast that which is good." (1 Th. 5:21). That being said, God willing, you will be brought to the proof and references you are seeking. As Jesus said, "…seek, and ye shall find…" (Matt. 7:7).

APPENDIX G

God's 7 day plan

Introduction

Moses was given, by God, three signs to show the Israelites that God was with him. The first was that when he threw down his rod, it would turn into a serpent, the second, was when he put his hand into his armpit and pulled it out again; it would turn leprous and when he put it in his armpit again and pulled it out it would be whole again and the third, was that when he poured out water taken from the river in a bowl onto the dry ground it would turn into blood (Ex. 4:1-9). These are three seemingly small miracles God showed Moses; but then we see these miracles being used similarly, on a greater scale, in front of Pharaoh, the people of Egypt and the Israelites in bondage there (Ex. 7:8-12, 14-25, 9:8-12). Also, these miraculous abilities could be transferred and duplicated, because God told Moses to instruct Aaron to throw down his rod in front of Pharaoh and his magicians and it turned into a serpent, theirs did the same, but Aarons rod ate them up (Ex. 7:8-12). Also, after the river was turned to blood using the rod that turned into a serpent; Moses asked Aaron to do the same to the streams, rivers and other bodies of water in Egypt, which he did, but God still takes credit for it all (Ex. 7:14-25). And last, a similar miracle happened regarding the leprosy of Moses' hand; he and Aaron tossed up ashes from the furnace into the air and the Egyptians and the beasts of the land began to develop boils, sores, upon their bodies (Ex. 9:8-12). I have had some similar examples in my life of miracles that have been shown to me, and I have mentioned most of them in my writing somewhere. Another example, I believe I have experienced is objects and living creatures appearing from seemingly nowhere. I am not positive about all of this, but as a young grown-up, when I first started attending church services again, reading the Holy Bible, repenting and praying, I noticed flies seemingly appear from nowhere. I do not know if this was a miracle of sorts or just a natural process, but I do remember thinking and I still do, where did these come from?

Of course, one of the ten plagues was lice coming up from the dust of the earth in the people of Egypt and in their beasts, and another was swarms of flies that came from somewhere (Ex 8:16-19, 20-32). But nevertheless, my main point is, that God reveals Himself to us, and He does it in such a way, to not overwhelm us. He reveals Himself to us a little bit at a time, and He does not do these things in vain; He reveals to us Himself, and then He uses those experiences to increase our faith (Rom. 1:17, 10:17; 2 Cor. 10:14-16, Eph. 2:8, 9; 2 Thess. 1:3, 4; Heb. 12:2, Jam. 1:2-4, 1 Pet. 1:6-9). So that if or when He decides to do greater miracles, like the ten plagues before the exodus of the Israelites from Egypt, or even the parting of the Red sea; at least we are somewhat aware of God's miraculous powers ahead of time, so we can act appropriately when He does things in a "bigger" way. Nevertheless, the remainder of this appendix is about God's seven day plan, expanding to a thousand years for each day, when we are looking at God's plan for this earth; from the creation week and Adam and Eve to the great white throne judgement before the "…new heaven and a new earth…" with the "…new Jerusalem…", that is to come (Gen. 1:1-2:3, Ps. 90:4, Rev. 20:11-15, Rev. 21:1, 2). The seven day week with a Sabbath rest on the seventh day is a sign, as much as all of the Holy days of God are, and it represents God's simple but overall plan for this current earth's history and all those whom inhabit it (Gen. 2:1-3). I have spoken of this idea in most of my writing and this appendix is meant to kind of bring it all together, as much as that is possible, summarizing why I have written my books. Read on to learn more. To God be the glory in the name of His only begotten Son, Jesus Christ of Nazareth. Alleluia and praise the LORD. Amen and Amen.

My people perish for lack of knowledge

Hosea 4:6 says, "My people are destroyed for lack of knowledge…". Proverbs 29:18 says, "Where *there is* no vision, the people perish…". The kingdom of God does not come by observation it is within us (Luke 17:20, 21). This is through receiving Jesus Christ of Nazareth as our Lord and Saviour, accepting His offering of the forgiveness of our sins by His Holy and righteous blood spilt on the cross for the forgiveness of our sins at Passover in 31 A.D.. Whom after His death on the cross was buried and three days later He arose to give us the hope and promise of eternal life in His Holy name. And He has given us of His Holy Spirit to dwell with us and in us, to comfort us and teach us, so that He is with us always, even to the end of the world and forever more in the "world to come" (John 14:16-18, 1 John 4:13). Alleluia and praise the LORD. Amen and Amen. Jesus Christ of Nazareth was conceived by the Holy Ghost, the Holy Spirit, in and born of the virgin, Mary, espoused to Joseph (Matt. 1:18-25). He was raised a child of Israel, of the tribe of Judah, with brothers and sisters (Matt. 13:55, 56; Luke 2:41-52, Rev. 5:5). He started His ministry at about the age of thirty and for three and a half years; He taught, healed, fed, and forgave us our sins, before His death on the cross for the forgiveness of our sins at Passover in 31 A.D., shedding His Holy and righteous blood (Luke 3:23, Matt. 27:33-28:10). He was buried and He arose the third day for the hope and promise of eternal life in His Holy name. He did this in obedience to God, the Father, through His Holy Spirit, that lighted upon Him at His baptism, like a dove, in the fall of 27 A.D.; about three and a half years before His crucifixion at Passover in 31 A.D. (Matt. 3:14-17, Luke. 3:21, 22). Jesus Christ of Nazareth is the "Word of God", and He was with God, the Father, in the beginning (John 1:1). And Jesus Christ of Nazareth and God, the Father, are one (John 10:30). Alleluia and praise the LORD. Amen and Amen.

Haggai 2:6 and 7 say, "For thus saith the LORD of hosts; Yet once, it *is* a little while, and I will shake the heavens, and the earth, and the sea, and the dry *land;* And I will shake all nations, and the desire of all nations shall come: and I will fill this house with glory, saith the LORD of hosts.". This has both spiritual and physical repercussions, firstly in Jesus Christ of Nazareth as Messiah, as the earth shook at His giving up of the ghost on the cross, and then after His resurrection, at the removing of the stone from His tomb (Matt. 27:51-53, 28:2). But this may have everything to do with the "Great Tribulation", that may still be yet to come on this world, as of the date of writing this book in 2019 A.D. (Matt. 24). As Jesus and other prophets of the Holy Bible have prophesied of, and I wrote a book about it called, "Time, Times and a dividing of Time – What did John really see?". Nevertheless, our reality is in Jesus Christ of Nazareth. Angels and the multitude of the heavenly host said of Jesus at the revelation to the shepherds of Jesus' birth, likely in the autumn of 4 B.C., "Glory to God in the highest, and on earth peace, good will towards men." (Luke 2:14). For the "Messianic age" and peace, in general, in this world; forgiveness is the key, and we have it and can give it in the name and strength of Jesus Christ of Nazareth. He died on the cross for the forgiveness of our sins at Passover in 31 A.D., spilling His Holy and righteous blood on the cross. He was buried, and the third day He arose to give us the hope and promise of eternal life in His Holy name. Alleluia and praise the LORD. Amen and Amen.

Accuracy

Matthew 24:36 and 37 say, "But of the day and hour knoweth no *man,* no, not the angels of heaven, but my Father only. But as the days of Noe *were,* so shall also the coming of the Son of man be.". Acts 1:6 and 7 says, "When they therefore were come together, they asked him, saying, Lord, wilt thou at this time restore again the kingdom of Israel? And he said unto them, It is not for you to know the times or the seasons, which the Father hath put in his own power.". As mentioned in chapter one, the earthly history of time keeping has become dependent on two systems; one using the sun, and the other using the moon. That being said, these two systems are not necessarily mutually exclusive; as at the least, it is the sun's light that reflects off of the moon and gives the moon its light (Isa. 30:26). Genesis 1:14-19 says, "And God said, Let there be lights in the firmament of the heaven to divide the day from the night; and let them be for signs, and for seasons, and for days, and years: And let them be for lights in the firmament of the heaven to give light upon the earth: and it was so. And God made two great lights; the greater light to rule the day, and the lesser light to rule the night: *he made* the stars also. And God set them in the firmament of the heaven to give light upon the earth, And to rule over the day and over the night, and to divide the light from the darkness: and God saw that *it was* good. And the evening and the morning were the fourth day.". It is also important to note, "It is the spirit that quickeneth; the flesh profiteth nothing..." (John 6:63). And God inhabits our praise, eternity; and He also has ultimate authority over the sun, moon and stars (Ps. 22:3, Isa. 57:15, Rev. 4:11). As the Bible says, "Thou art worthy, O Lord, to receive glory and honour and power: for thou hast created all things..." (John 1:1-3, Rev. 4:11). We must also keep in mind; that it is His Holy Spirit that reveals to us all things, through God, the Father's, only begotten Son, Jesus Christ of Nazareth (John 14:26, 1 John 2:27). Alleluia and praise the LORD. Amen and Amen.

Also, blindness has a purpose (Ezek. 39:22-29, Rom. 11:25). The Bible would even suggest a blind person is perfect. Isaiah 42:19 says, "Who *is* blind, but my servant? or deaf, as my messenger *that* I sent? Who *is* blind as *he that* is perfect, and blind as the LORD's servant?". Jesus said, "...if ye were blind: ye should have no sin..." (John 9:41). That being said, we should not physically blind ourselves, but we need to seek God's knowledge and desires for us, instead of our own desires (Matt. 6:22, 23; 18:9). And last, we have the love of Christ that passes knowledge, and the peace of God that passes all understanding (Eph. 3:19, Phil. 4:7). Another note regarding prophecy and its accuracy; is that even during a time of relative peace, and prophesying about building toward peace and working towards a common goal of peace, trouble can still come and be prophesied to come. Zechariah in particular is a good example of this. He was prophesying about the time of the building and completion of the second temple around 481 to 477 B.C., but he also prophesied of future events at that time, regarding the "...day of the LORD..." (Zech. 14:1-3). Of course, this was fulfilled in Christ's time spiritually, because of the division Jesus caused amongst the people, and His day on the cross at Passover in 31 A.D. (Luke 12:51). But also the temple was physically destroyed in 70 A.D. by the Romans and Jerusalem was "spoiled", according to historical references.[20] Also, Jerusalem has been a "...cup of trembling..." and a "...burdensome stone..." to the nations from time to time, as prophesied (Zech. 12:2, 3). But also, this may speak of the "Great Tribulation", which as of the date of writing this book in 2019 A.D., may not have taken place yet fully (Matt. 24). Nevertheless, the reality is in Jesus Christ of Nazareth, whom has taken on Himself, the wrath of God, on the cross for the forgiveness of our sins. He died on the cross for the forgiveness of our sins, spilling His Holy and righteous blood at Passover in 31

---

[20] https://www.britannica.com/event/Siege-of-Jerusalem-70, retrieved 27/04/2022

A.D.. He was buried and the third day He arose to give us the hope and promise of eternal like in His Holy name. Alleluia and praise the LORD. Amen and Amen.

While working on the main body of this book and a couple others before it, I decided to seriously commit myself to using the Holy Bible to show me with whatever evidence I could find, the most accurate dating of all of the events in the Holy Bible that I could possibly find. I used references by the apostle, Paul, in the New Testament, and most if not all of the references of chronology that come from the Old Testament. I came up with a dating from about 4000 B.C. for the beginning with the creation week and Adam and Eve, making the year 2000 the six thousandth year of man's current history here on earth. Of course, we had the Y2K panic in the year two thousand, but because of preparation or otherwise, the start of the so called "new millennia" had no notable epic disasters. I am not the only person that has come up with this approximate dating, and there have been at least a few suggestions of when certain Biblical prophecy would be fulfilled regarding the "Great Tribulation", and other major "end-time" events that are mentioned in the Holy Bible. Nevertheless, the reality is, Jesus said that we do not know the day or hour, as I have mentioned more than once in my writing. He says that we ought to watch and pray, we do not know if He is coming at the first, second, third, or fourth watch or in the day time (Matt. 24:20, 21, 42; Luke 12:37-39). And the reality is, He also said that the kingdom of God does not come by observation but that it is within us (Luke 17:20, 21). If or when the "Great Tribulation" comes, for three and a half years, and the "Messianic Age" begins right after it; God only knows for certain, as of the date of writing this book in 2019 A.D.. But as I have mentioned He does desire us to be ready for things to come, and He prepares us for them. Alleluia and praise the LORD. Amen and Amen.

I would suggest that my interpretation of Biblical chronology is as accurate as I could possibly interpret using the Holy Bible, and I would suggest there is likely room for a margin of error in my general chronological interpretation by about one hundred years. And I am rather convinced that some of the dating I have written about; namely of Jesus conception, birth, death and resurrection are truly accurate. This all being said, the seemingly common "Jewish" chronology of Biblical history sets us in the 5778th year from the beginning of the creation, as of the year, 2018 A.D. (Gen. 1:1-2:4). Again this is an interpretation and would be about two hundred and forty years different from my estimates using the Holy Bible as the reference. But just like everything I or anyone else has written or interpreted about God and His works; the call is, as the apostle, Paul, says, "…let God be true, but every man a liar…" (Rom. 3:4). Alleluia and praise the LORD. Amen and Amen. So our reality ought to be in God, the Father, and Jesus Christ of Nazareth, His only begotten Son, through His Holy Spirit given to us. It is His Holy Spirit that teaches us all things and reveals to us things to come, as the testimony of Jesus Christ of Nazareth is the spirit of prophecy (John 14:26, 1 John 2:27, Rev. 19:10). Alleluia and praise the LORD. Most importantly, Jesus Christ of Nazareth died on the cross for the forgiveness of our sins at Passover in 31 A.D., and He shed His Holy and righteous blood on the cross. He was buried and the third day He arose to give us the hope and promise of eternal life in His Holy name. Alleluia and praise the LORD. Amen and Amen.

Plan

God has a plan and He has been working it out here on earth with man for almost 6,000 years. If we use God's principle of one day is a thousand years to God, we are likely nearing the 7th day or

1000 years of rest, as of the date of writing this book in 2019 A.D. (Ps. 90:4, 2 Pet. 3:8, Rev. 20:4). Now, why is nearly all of Christianity and the rest of the world oblivious to this truth? The so called god of this "world", that is Satan, and his followers have deceived us with false doctrines and feast days (John 14:30, Rev. 12:9). Actually, the Israelites that rebelled against God before they went into captivity around three thousand years ago, namely by Jeroboam, the king of Israel at the time, initiated this change of days of worship and location, because of his concern of losing control of the northern tribes of Israel during his reign (1 Kings 12:26-33). The Danites started this worshipping of idols even before that, mentioned in the book of Judges, as I had given account of in my book, "The Origins of Mankind", and elsewhere in my writings (Jud. 18). Nevertheless, God's weekly Sabbath, the seventh day of the week, and His annual Holy days are a sign, a shadow of good things to come and are an outright message of remembrance, blessing and warning for those whom keep them (Gen. 2:2, 3; Lev. 23, Ps. 19:7-11, Col. 2:16, 17; Heb. 10:1). They are a reminder of the past, a blessing for the present, and a hope for the future. The first indication of God's message in "time" is that of the creation week account (Gen. 1:1-2:3). Six days God spent working on the creation of the heavens and the earth, and all that are in them, and on the seventh day He rested (Gen. 1-2:3). The seventh day was established as a day of rest, not only that, but He blessed and sanctified it, not only on the first week of creation, but for every week after that during mankind's sojourn here on earth (Gen. 2:3, Ex. 20:9, 10). As even Jesus said, the Son of man is even Lord of the Sabbath day (Matt. 12:8). And "...The sabbath was made for man..." (Mark 2:27, 28). We were created to work, but God also created the Sabbath for us to rest in (Gen. 1:26-29, 2:2, 3). Alleluia and praise the LORD. Amen and Amen.

Now as was mentioned earlier, in 2 Peter 3:8, a day can represent or have a likeness of 1000 years, also mentioned in Psalm 90. This next part takes some understanding, but using the Bible, we can calculate from the beginning with Adam and Eve unto today, using ages of peoples birth and death, amounts of time of people being in ruling power, and other more recent historical records, that we are indeed near this 6000 year mark, as of the date of writing this book in 2019 A.D., as mentioned in the previous section (Gen. 5, 11, 21:5, 25:20, etc.). God has made a plan for mankind indeed. He has allowed us to work with Him for almost 6000 years now. But we are most certainly nearing the final 1000 years of rest; that God has promised to those whom obey Him (Rev. 20:4, 6). Alleluia and praise the LORD. Amen and Amen. This seventh day of rest command was reaffirmed during Israel's sojourn in the wilderness. They were to collect manna six days, and collect extra on the sixth day so that they could rest on the seventh day and still have enough manna to eat (Ex. 16). Along with this physical example of not working on the seventh day, came the same message from Mount Sinai in the 10 commandments (Ex. 20:9, 10). Later again, reaffirmed in the books of the law and throughout the Old Testament in synagogues and at the Temple in Jerusalem; this continued even in Jesus' time and into the New Testament Church after His ascension (Lev. 23:3, Mark 1:21, Acts 13:14). And it continues even to today, through various Christian and Jewish organizations that have kept or renewed their desire to keep, the commands of God, especially the command to rest weekly on the seventh day and keep it holy (Gen. 2:2, 3). You can partake in this command too. If you do, God promises, you will be blessed for it (Deut. 28:1-14). Obedience to God brings forth blessing. Why not try it out and experience it with God, the Father, Almighty, in Christ Jesus of Nazareth's Holy name, God's only begotten Son, with His Holy Spirit and with whom else God wills it. To learn more of God's Holy days read Leviticus 23, in the Holy Bible of God. Alleluia and praise the LORD. Amen and Amen.

Conclusion

No matter the truth of all of these ideas of when things have happened in the past, or when things may come to pass looking forward. We need to consider and place our trust in our Creator, through Jesus Christ of Nazareth, today. God is not a God afar off, He is very near to us, the Holy Bible even says His word is in our mouth and heart (Deut. 30:14). He does indeed give us our very breath of life (Gen. 2:7). As Jesus said of Himself, "...Before Abraham was, I am." (John 8:58). He is ever present, everlasting, and everywhere. It may be important for us to understand in some detail the possibilities of things to come, but our reality still needs to be in Jesus Christ of Nazareth. God has created all things, and created them for His pleasure (John 1:1-3, Rev. 4:11). He directs our steps, and establishes our thoughts (Jer. 10:23, Amos 4:13). He has given us life, and He will take us to where He is when it is our time (John 14:1-4). One of the more important reasons for my having studied and found a multitude of evidence, albeit, not all one hundred percent agreeable regarding the truth of the Holy Bible, is just that; God through the apostle, Paul, admonishes, "Prove all things; hold fast that which is good." (1 Thess. 5:21). So in my writing, I have attempted to do this, writing about history, contemporary concerns, prophecy and finding proof I had not even imagined I would ever find, never mind thought I would write about. But God through His miraculous abilities has revealed it both to me, namely through His Holy Bible by His Holy Spirit, and to and through the references I have found, and I am sure to you and other references that I have not even known about. But again the reality is in Jesus Christ of Nazareth. Alleluia and praise the LORD. He was indeed conceived by the Holy Spirit of God in and born of the virgin, Mary, espoused to Joseph (Matt. 1:18-25). He was raised as a child of Israel, of the tribe of Judah (Luke 2:41-52, Rev. 5:5). At about the age of thirty He began His earthly ministry and for three and a half years; He did miracles, He healed, He forgave sins and ultimately He died on the cross for the forgiveness of our sins at Passover in 31 A.D., shedding His Holy and righteous blood on the cross for the forgiveness of our sins (Luke 3:23). He was buried and the third day He arose to give us the hope and promise of eternal life in His Holy name. Alleluia and praise the LORD. Amen and Amen.

Reader's Guide

This book was written with the idea of order in mind. There may be some subjects in the end that are of more interest, or need more clarification, where you may desire to review them for a better understanding. Part of the reason why the "appendices" exist is to expand on some of the topics written about in this book, so referring to them may be preferred. When writing the book I had in mind I was reaching out to a "lost" generation, but the truth of the matter is we are all children of God, no matter what age we are. Some of the topics discussed are not usually talked about at least commonly, weekly, in Church or in the home, at least that I know of, so they may be new to the reader. And it may take some time to discern how to apply them to each of our daily lives.

The question section attempts to do this, at least in part, by opening back up the readers mind to the Holy Spirit of God. So that you can pray about, meditate on and discuss with others the subjects spoken about. Although the topics in this book have been spoken about and continue to be spoken about by various students of the Holy Bible, the reality of the subjects will only be fully known in God's timing. In order to better understand our place with God, in life, family and in this world, we need to grow in our understanding of somethings. Hopefully, most of the subjects will be simple enough to understand that not much contemplation is needed, because God does desire us to become like little children in our relationship with Him and others (Matt. 18:3). So with that being said, pray about, meditate on and discuss the ideas that interest you with whom God wills and see if you can come to some peace in these matters. God bless and keep the faith!

Chapter One: In the beginning

Discussion: Time

"O LORD, I know that the way of man *is* not in himself: *it is*
not in man that walketh to direct his steps."
- Jeremiah 10:23

When I was considering my options and under review, during my last six month in the military, amongst other things, I had picked up the Bible that had been given to me by a relative in University. I had read up to 1 Chronicles in University, but the list of names became too tedious and boring for me to continue reading, so I stopped reading it. I know now, that the seemingly tedious and boring stuff in the Holy Bible is as important, as the more "interesting" passages. It is just that we all have a time for understanding and requiring certain knowledge about things in this world, so I suppose it was not my time to continue reading the Bible, at that time. At any rate, I started reading the Bible again in late 2009, early 2010 A.D., and I must have come to the passage above, or else I just randomly flipped to it. The situation was such, that I drove my vehicle, at the time, to a local conservation area on the outskirts of the town I was living in, and I walked some distance through the trails and into the woods for some peace and quiet. I took this Bible I was reading, from University, with me; it was the New International Version, for the reader's information. I sat down under a tree and flipped to Jeremiah 10:23, although I may have been reading other verses at the time, I do not remember. Nevertheless, my attention was drawn to Jeremiah 10:23, and I kept reading it over and over again, the sun was just above the tree line in the distance, in the west, and it was around winter time, as there were a few centimeters of snow on the ground. At the time, the meaning of the verse did not mean that much to me, but I must have repeated it so many times that it has been etched into my memory. It has served me well in remembering that God is indeed sovereign over all things, and it is a reminder that both the New Testament and the Old Testament agree on this. Alleluia and praise the LORD. Amen and Amen.

Discussion Questions

1. Is Jesus the Messiah, the Saviour of the world, and the prophesied eternal King over Israel?

   a. Proverbs 29:14 says, "The king that faithfully judgeth the poor, his throne shall be established forever.". Who fulfilled this verse? David or Jesus or someone else? Jesus Christ of Nazareth did! Alleluia and praise the LORD. Amen and Amen.

   b. The Scriptures confirm that Jesus Christ of Nazareth is the Messiah, the "anointed", Christ means anointed (Luke 4:16-21).

   c. The Bible says without faith we cannot please God; this includes having faith in the truth of whom Jesus Christ of Nazareth is. Faith is a gift from God (Eph. 2:8, 9).

   d. Ultimately we all need to take that step of faith ourselves and choose what we believe. I know I did. So what are you waiting for? Ask God for the faith to believe the truth! He will not lie to you! Put your trust in Him and let Him reveal to you the truth of whom Jesus Christ of Nazareth is! What do you have to loose?

e. Proverbs 28:26 says, "He that trusteth in his own heart is a fool...". So where is your trust? Whom do you place your trust in? Have faith and live! Christ Jesus of Nazareth is the answer!

2. Hate and the sword and division are all mentioned by Jesus in His ministry, mostly in reference to family, although He did mention that His followers would be hated by all (Matt. 10:22). The question is then, what did He mean in these various circumstances, and how does that "hate" affect our lives here on earth?

    a. Love your enemy (Matt. 5:44).
    b. Jesus comes first, before all else; we cannot receive salvation from the spirit or body of anyone else. Not our spouse, not our children and not from any other here on earth. Some may be able to show us God's love and teach us about the truth; but God, the Father, in Jesus Christ of Nazareth, through forgiveness of our sins, and receiving His Holy Spirit as a promise is the Saviour of us all. Alleluia and praise the LORD. Amen and Amen.

Chapter Two: The Sabbath

Discussion: Sabbath

> "For the LORD thy God walketh in the midst of thy camp, to deliver thee,
> and to give up thine enemies before thee; therefore shall thy camp be holy:
> that he see no unclean thing in thee, and turn away from thee."
> - Deuteronomy 23:14

It should be mentioned that the apostle, Paul, mentions, "For all have sinned and come short of the glory of God.", as is similarly mentioned in two Old Testament Psalms (Ps. 14:1, 3; 53:1, 3; Rom. 3:23). That being said, Jesus also admonishes us to be perfect, even as our Father in Heaven is perfect (Matt. 5:48). He also says, that if our righteousness does not exceed that of the scribes and Pharisees, we will not enter into the kingdom of God (Matt. 5:20). This is why the Bible can be interpreted, and why various scholars have speculated about the validity of, any one translation of the Holy Bible of God. That being said, if we truly believe there is a God, and that He is the Creator, then we need not worry or be anxious about interpretations, translations, etc.. Jesus said that He, Himself, is the way, the truth and the life (John 14:6). If He is the truth, and He has given us His Holy Spirit, which is truthful, then God, the Father, through His Holy Spirit, in the name of His only begotten Son, Jesus Christ of Nazareth, will lead us into all truth, as Jesus said (John 16:13). The truth is that in order for Deuteronomy 23:14 above to be fulfilled, we need Jesus Christ of Nazareth. He is the only man, conceived by the Holy Spirit of God, in and born to the virgin, Mary, espoused to Joseph, of the tribe of Judah, of the house of David, born a sinless man (Matt. 1:18-25, Rev. 5:5). He had brothers and sisters, and was raised as a child of Israel (Matt. 13:55, 56; Luke 2:41-52). He began His ministry at the age of about thirty years old and for three and a half years, did miracles, preached, ministered, healed and forgave sins, as a sinless man (Luke 3:23). And at Passover in 31 A.D., He died on the cross for the forgiveness of our sins, shedding His Holy and righteous blood. He was buried and the third day He arose to give us the hope and promise of eternal life in His Holy name. Alleluia and praise the LORD. Amen and Amen.

Discussion Questions

1. The knowledge of all of these different signs and the Holy Days of God are great, and ought to be followed, if done in the Spirit of Jesus Christ of Nazareth. But what is the reality of all of this?

   a. The reality is in Christ.
   b. Common salvation (Jude 3).
   c. Jew and Gentile believers in Christ have a common salvation in Jesus Christ of Nazareth. This is why He came, to simplify the interpretations and traditions surrounding the actual law. He did not come to destroy it. He came to fulfil, rather, complete the law!
   4. What about idols? What can they teach us?
   e. Habakkuk 2:18-20.
   f. Nothing.

Chapter Three: Passover and Feast of Unleavened Bread

Discussion: Passover

"By the which will we are sanctified through the offering
of the body of Jesus Christ once *for all*."
- Hebrews 10:10

Jesus Christ of Nazareth said on the cross, "...My God, my God, why hast thou forsaken me?" (Matt. 27:46). I have addressed this question in a few places in my writing, but I will speak of it from a different perspective here. Jesus cast out a devil from a boy that was dumb and deaf (Mark 9:25). I heard once that Satan is very intelligent, but if we know somebody by their fruits, then how could Satan be intelligent (Matt. 7:16)? Nevertheless, similar to this boy, Jesus seems to have manifested the complete separation from God by taking all of our sin upon Himself on the cross (Matt. 27:46). The apostle, Paul, even said God made Jesus to be sin who knew no sin (2 Cor. 5:21). The point is, that Jesus Christ of Nazareth suffered much in order for us to be saved. He was crowned with a crown of thorns (Matt. 27:29, Mark 15:17, John 19:1). And the apostle, Paul, had a thorn in the flesh, the messenger of Satan to humble him, but God said, "My grace is sufficient for thee..." (2 Cor. 12:7-9). In weakness, God's strength is perfected, and of course this goes for any of us, including our Saviour Jesus Christ of Nazareth, whose weakness was an earthly death on the cross for the forgiveness of our sins (2 Cor. 12:9). Nevertheless, in both the New and Old Testament, I have come across at least a few of what some may consider, "contradictions", between various disciples accounts of how Jesus lived His life, and how these disciples recorded them either first hand or by eyewitness account (Luke 1:1-4). I have done some thought about all of this, and I think the crown of thorns describes this whole situation well. The Holy Bible of God, and life in some respects can seem to be a crown of thorns, when we are persecuted, commit sin and are punished, when we are struggling with understanding of what God is doing, and saying through His Word, the Holy Bible and how He desires us to live this life (Job 31:35, 36). But ultimately, we must place our trust in the true God, the living God, through Jesus Christ of Nazareth. Whom died on the cross for the forgiveness of our sins at Passover in 31 A.D., shedding His Holy and righteous blood on the cross. He was buried and the third day He arose again to give us the hope and promise of eternal life in His Holy name. Alleluia and praise the LORD. The apostle, Paul, speaks of the love of Christ that passes knowledge, and the peace of God that passes understanding (Eph. 3:19, Phil. 4:7). So just like our failures in sin, which bring us to death, so to through Jesus Christ of Nazareth, are we redeemed to our Creator, God, the Father, through His only begotten Son, Jesus Christ of Nazareth. Alleluia and praise the LORD. And He has given us of His Holy Spirit to dwell in and with us forever (1 John 4:13). Jesus Christ of Nazareth and God, the Father, through His Holy Spirit are with us forever (Matt. 28:20). Alleluia and praise the LORD. Amen and Amen. When reading through this section's discussions consider your relationship with your Creator, in Christ Jesus of Nazareth, and how He desires you to live out the remainder of your life here on earth, and in the "world to come", eternal life. Alleluia and praise the LORD. Amen and Amen.

Discussion Questions

1. What is the appropriate age to learn the deeper things of God?

   a. Ministers begin ministering at age 50 (Num. 8:25, 26)
   b. Work in the tabernacle starts at age 30 to age 50 (Num. 4:3)
   c. Levites wait on service of tabernacle at age 25 to age 50 (Num. 8:24, 25)
   d. Men of Israel are counted, starting at age 20 (Num. 1:3)
   e. Offerings are required starting at age 20 (Ex. 30:14, 38:26)
   f. Jeremiah (Jer. 1:6).
   g. Elihu (Job 32:4-10).
   h. Out of the mouth of babes God has ordained strength and perfected praise (Ps. 8:2, Matt. 21:16).
   i. Ultimately God is the best teacher (Ps. 34:11, 119:108, 132:12).
   j. Jesus was prophesied of and honoured by the angel of the LORD, in the dream of Joseph and in a vision of Mary, warning of His Holy Spirit conceived birth in the virgin, Mary, espoused to Joseph (Matt. 1:20, 21; Luke 1:26-38). Jesus was honoured again by the angel in heaven to the Shepherds in the field, and then witnessed by the Shepherds in Judea, at His birth (Luke 2:8-17). Jesus was honoured and worshipped as a King by the wise men from the east, at about the age of two years old (Matt. 2:1-11). And at age twelve, Jesus was in the temple speaking with the religious authorities, and He had knowledge (Luke 2:41-52). And Jesus started His earthly ministry at the age of about thirty years old for three and a half years (Luke 3:23). And after this, He died on the cross for the forgiveness of our sins at Passover in 31 A.D., spilling His Holy and righteous blood on the cross. He was buried and He arose again the third day to give us the hope and promise of eternal life in His Holy name. Alleluia and praise the LORD. Amen and Amen.

2. What about nature? Can we learn from God's creation outside of the Bible and the Holy Spirit working through other people?

   a. Job 12:7, 8
   b. Nature is proof of God's existence (Job 12:8).
   c. Ultimately, God is the best teacher (Ps.32:8).

3. Can we learn from the memories and experiences of our ancestors whom have passed before us?

   a. Job 8:8-10
   b. We may have been given examples of how to treat others, or how to conduct our behaviour, or how to conduct healthy conversation from our relatives whom have passed.
   c. Ultimately, God is the best teacher (Ps. 25:4, 5, 8, 9, 12).

Chapter Four: Pentecost

Discussion: Firstfruits

> "...freely ye have received, freely give."
> - Matthew 10:8

The Holy Bible speaks of giving our firstfruits to God, tithing and being a cheerful giver (Ex. 23:19, Lev. 27:30, 2 Cor. 9:7). The apostle, Paul, spoke of husbandman, that labour, being first partaker of the fruits (2 Tim. 2:6). I suppose this could be his way of encouraging a savings of some sorts. For practical reasons probably, because God desired the church of God, and the congregation to have a certain degree of independence from the governing system of that time, and whatever social welfare programs they had. The same is still relevant for us today. Of course, financial investment institutions teach to save the first ten percent for ourselves. But no matter, as 1 Chronicles 29:14 says of God, "...all things *come* of thee, and of thine own have we given thee.". That is, the reality is, that all our money, possessions, lands, etc., ultimately belong to the Creator, God, the Father, Almighty, whom created all things (John 1:3, Rev. 4:11). He has given us the earth, and He has given it to us to inhabit, and even have dominion over, but this requires obedience to Him, first and foremost (Gen. 1:28). And more importantly, Jesus Christ of Nazareth said of Himself that "...All power is given unto me in heaven and in earth." (Matt. 28:18). So the reality is, that everything we have, do and see, come from our Creator, in the name of His only begotten Son, Jesus Christ of Nazareth, whom died on the cross for the forgiveness of our sins at Passover in 31 A.D., shedding His Holy and righteous blood for us. He was buried and on the third day He arose to give us the hope and promise of eternal life in His Holy name. Alleluia and praise the LORD. Amen and Amen. Jesus said "...Make to yourselves friends of the mammon of unrighteousness; that, when ye fail, they may receive you into everlasting habitations." (Luke 16:9). Two examples come to mind when thinking about what Jesus is saying; the first is that He miraculously had a coin appear in the mouth of a fish for Peter to use to pay the tribute to the tribute money collector (Matt. 17:24-27). And the widow's mite, is the second example, whom Jesus said, cast more into the treasury out of her penury, than all that the rich men had cast in out of there abundance (Mark 12:41-44). So again, this is the reality we have in Jesus Christ of Nazareth; that He is a miracle worker, and that giving when we think we have next to nothing, is a much greater gift then giving abundantly, out of abundance. This is why Jesus said, "Blessed are the poor in spirit..." (Matt. 5:3). And why He spoke of faith as a mustard seed (Matt. 17:20). Alleluia and praise the LORD. Amen and Amen.

Discussion Questions

1. The Bible speaks in many places of the traps, snares and pits that the enemy creates for us. What can you do to avoid these pitfalls in life? What does the Bible say about those who create these pits?

   a. Be vigilant (Matt. 24:42).
   b. Pray always (1 Thess. 5:17).
   c. Turn the other cheek (Matt. 5:39).
   d. Those who create the pit will fall into it (Ps. 7:15).

e. Psalm 69
f. Book of Esther example

2. What is required of us to be teachers of God's truth? (Hint: Psalm 51:11-13)

    a. Psalm 51:11-13 says, "Cast me not away from thy presence; and take not thy Holy Spirit from me. Restore unto me the joy of thy salvation; and uphold me *with thy* free spirit. *Then* will I teach transgressors thy ways; and sinners shall be converted unto thee.".
    b. We need the Holy Spirit in us to teach others of God's truth; also, we need to have the joy of the salvation message! Alleluia and praise the LORD. Amen and Amen.
    c. One of the fruits of God's Holy Spirit is joy. The others are "...love...peace, longsuffering, gentleness, goodness, faith, Meekness, temperance: against such there is no law." (Gal. 5:22, 23).

3. Who is the ultimate teacher?

    a. Psalm 119:99 says, "I have more understanding than all my teachers: for thy testimonies *are* my meditation.".
    b. 1 John 2:27 says, "But the anointing which ye have received of him abideth in you, and ye need not that any man teach you: but as the same anointing teacheth you of all things, and is truth, and is no lie, and even as it hath taught you, ye shall abide in him.".
    c. Acts 2:17 says, "And it shall come to pass in the last days, saith God, I will pour out my Spirit upon all flesh..." (Joel 2:28).
    d. Jeremiah 31:34 says, "And they shall teach no more every man his neighbour, and every man his brother, saying, Know the LORD: for they shall all know me, from the least of them unto the greatest of them, saith the LORD: for I will forgive their iniquity, and I will remember their sin no more.". Alleluia and praise the LORD. Amen and Amen.
    e. This was ultimately confirmed by Jesus Christ of Nazareth, whom said He would send the Comforter, the Holy Ghost, to us, after His resurrection and His ascension into a cloud in heaven (Acts 1:1-9). Jesus is the Comforter (John 14:16-18). And He dwells in us, as we receive Him, the only begotten Son of God, with God, the Father, Almighty, through His Holy Spirit. He was conceived by the Holy Spirit of God in and born of the virgin, Mary, espoused to Joseph (Matt. 1:18-25). He was raised, a child of Israel, of the tribe of Judah, with brothers and sisters (Matt. 13:55, 56; Luke 2:41-52, Rev. 5:5). He began His earthly ministry at about the age of thirty in 27 A.D., and He taught, healed, forgave and did other miracles for three and a half years (Luke 3:23). And at Passover in 31 A.D., He died on the cross for the forgiveness of our sins, shedding His Holy and righteous blood on the cross. He was buried and the third day He arose to give us the hope and promise of eternal life in His Holy name. Alleluia and praise the LORD. Amen and Amen.

Chapter Five: Feast of Trumpets and Day of Atonement

Discussion: Salvation in Christ Jesus of Nazareth

> "...do not sound a trumpet before thee..."
> - Matthew 6:2

The book of Joel goes into greater detail about the "great tribulation", and speaks about Jehoshaphat and the valley of decision. The reality is, we all have decisions to make in this life, whether they are simple daily ones, or potentially life changing ones. Jehoshaphat was a king of Judah, and he followed the Lord (1 Kings 22:42-44). One time, the people of Moab and Ammon, descendants of Lot, and people of mount Seir, came to battle Jehoshaphat and the people of the cities of Judah (2 Chr. 20:1). So Jehoshaphat proclaimed a fast and consulted with God about what to do (2 Chr. 20:3-13). Through Jahaziel, a Levite, of the children of Asaph, God said go up to the battle, but the battle would be God's to fight (2 Chr. 20:14-17). Jehoshaphat and his people went up to the battle and stood ready, and they simply praised God (2 Chr. 20:18-22). Miraculously the Moabites and the Ammonites turned on the army of mount Seir and destroyed them, and then turned on one another, and destroyed one another (2 Chr. 20:23). This is the simple and yet truly effective way of "winning" our battles here on earth, first and foremost, in the spiritual realm. That is we ought to worship the true God only, and serve Him only, first and foremost, and then He will take care of the rest. Jesus said, "But the hour cometh, and now is, when the true worshippers shall worship the Father in spirit and in truth: for the Father seeketh such to worship him.". (John 4:23). We must continually remember that Jesus Christ of Nazareth is the way, the truth and the life (John 14:6). And there is no other name under heaven whereby we can be saved (Acts 4:12). That is, Jesus Christ of Nazareth came for us, while we were yet sinners. He was conceived by the Holy Spirit in and born of the virgin, Mary, espoused to Joseph (Matt. 1:18-25). He was raised a child of Israel, of the tribe of Judah, of the house of David, with brothers and sisters (Matt. 13:55, 56; Luke 2:41-52, Rev. 5:5). He healed, He taught us about all things, and did other miracles, and promised us that He would always be with us through His Holy Spirit (Matt. 28:20, Mark 13:23, John 14:16-18, 26). Alleluia and praise the LORD. Amen and Amen. And most importantly, He spilt His righteous and holy blood on the cross for the forgiveness of our sins and died on the cross at Passover in 31 A.D.. He was buried and the third day He arose, giving us the hope and promise of eternal life in His Holy name. Alleluia and praise the LORD. Amen and Amen.

Discussion Questions

1. What is knowledge, wisdom and understanding?

    a. The fear of the Lord is the beginning of wisdom (Prov. 9:10).
    b. Knowledge of the Holy is understanding (Prov. 9:10)
    c. The peace of God, in Jesus Christ of Nazareth, passes all understanding (Phil. 4:7).

2. How do we come to learn the deeper things of God?

   a. Isaiah 28:9 says, "Whom shall he teach knowledge? and whom shall he make to understand doctrine? *them that are* weaned from the milk, *and* drawn from the breasts.".

   b. Salvation comes from faith in Jesus Christ of Nazareth. He was conceived by the Holy Spirit of God, in and born of the virgin, Mary, espoused to Joseph (Matt. 1:18-25). He was raised, a child of Israel, of the tribe of Judah, with brothers and sisters (Matt. 13:55, 56; Luke 2:41-42, Rev. 5:5). At the age of about thirty, He began His earthly ministry; forgiving, healing, and doing other miracles, for three and a half years (Luke 3:23). And at Passover in 31 A.D., He died on the cross for the forgiveness of sins, shedding His Holy and righteous blood on the cross. He was buried and the third day He arose for the hope and promise of eternal life in His Holy name. This is the true milk of God (1 Pet. 2:2, 3). Alleluia and praise the LORD. Amen and Amen.

   c. The deeper things of God; the doctrines, the commands, the Holy Days, etc.; these are the meat. Just like meat helps strengthen our muscles and helps us grow, the meat of God helps strengthen our spiritual muscles and helps us grow in our relationship with God, the Father, Almighty with Jesus Christ of Nazareth, through His Holy Spirit, and with others here on earth. Alleluia and praise the LORD. Amen and Amen.

Chapter Six: Feast of Tabernacles and the Last Great Day

Discussion: The Grace of God

> "For by grace are ye saved through faith; and that not of yourselves: *it is* the gift of God: Not of works, lest any man should boast."
> - Ephesians 2:8, 9

God, through Moses, speaks in Deuteronomy 9 of Israel possessing the "promised land" of Canaan, after coming out of the wilderness. He says that the people of the land are great and tall, greater and mightier than the Israelites and the Israelites will possess their land (Deut. 9:1, 2). God says He will go before them as a consuming fire and destroy these nations and drive them out before the Israelites face (Deut. 9:3). Deuteronomy 9:4 and 5 say, "Speak not thou in thine heart, after that the LORD thy God hath cast them out from before thee, saying, For my righteousness the LORD hath brought me in to possess this land: but for the wickedness of these nations the LORD doth drive them out from before thee. Not for thy righteousness, or for the uprightness of thine heart, does thou go to possess their land: but for the wickedness of these nations the LORD thy God doth drive them out from before thee, and that he may perform the word which the LORD sware unto thy fathers, Abraham, Isaac, and Jacob.". In the proceeding versus Moses goes on to bring up the things Israel had done in the wilderness to provoke God to anger, and calls Israel a stiffnecked people (Deut. 9:6-26). The point is, that this verse of the Old Testament and part of the books of the law of God, are prophetic in nature, and speak of God's grace towards His called and chosen people. Jesus said of Himself, in the New Testament, "Think not that I am come to destroy the law, or the prophets: I am not come to destroy, but to fulfil." (Matt. 5:17). The apostle, Paul, speaks of the "… law of Christ…" (Gal. 6:2). The point is, that Jesus Christ of Nazareth is "…I AM…", and God does not change (Ex. 3:14, Isa. 43:13, Mal. 3:6, John 8:58). God, the Father, with His only begotten Son, Jesus Christ of Nazareth, the Word become flesh, and the Holy Ghost, were with the Israelites in the wilderness, they were with Abraham before that, and they were in the beginning before the day light was created (Gen. 1:2, Isa. 43:13, John 1:1, 14; 1 Cor. 10:4). So if there is to come a prophetic "Messianic Age", and the feast of tabernacles is a prophetic sign of the "Messianic Age" to come, as of the date of writing this book in 2019 A.D.; we need not be worried or concerned about our part in "making" it come to pass. It is God, the Father, Almighty, whom does the work in us and through us and around us through His Holy Spirit, the Holy Ghost; it is in Jesus Christ of Nazareth's Holy name we are saved, "Messianic Age" or no "Messianic Age". And the Holy Bible says of Jesus, "And when he was demanded of the Pharisees, when the kingdom of God should come, he answered them and said, The kingdom of God cometh not with observation: Neither shall they say, Lo here! or, lo there! for, behold, the kingdom of God is within you." (Luke 17:20, 21). Alleluia and praise the LORD. Amen and Amen. Read on to open your mind to whatever God wills you, regarding your relationship with Him today, the possibilities in the "Messianic Age", and forever more in the "world to come". Alleluia and praise the LORD. Amen and Amen.

Discussion Questions

1. God speaks of the power of our tongue; what changes can you make in your communication, to speak life into this world and others?

   a. Proverbs 16:20 – 24

2. In the "Messianic age", the Levites are restored to their position of authority in teaching the commands of God to the people. How might this change from today's world?

   a. Many Levites today are likely involved in the education system, lawyers, doctors, and other professionals. And no doubt there are Levites that are "Rabbi's" and possibly even Christian pastors today.
   b. The role may not change much, but the knowledge being taught may change to suit the realities of the time.
   c. Ezekiel 44:23, Micah 4:2
   d. However, we must understand that we do live in a fallen world today, as of the date of writing this book in 2019 A.D., and that ultimately we need to place our trust in Jesus Christ of Nazareth to be our teacher, in the Holy Spirit of God (Mic. 3:11).

Chapter Seven: Summaries and Conclusion

Discussion: Peace

> "Great peace have they which love thy law: and nothing shall offend them."
> - Psalm 119:165

In my later stages of writing my books, as I started writing the last five congruently, but finishing them separately, various Bible verses came into mind, that had been remembered from previous leisure reading. The idea of the fruits of the Holy Spirit, and Jesus commanding us not to blaspheme the Holy Spirit was paramount in my mind for at least a week (Mark 3:28, 29; Gal. 5:22, 23). The point is, that one of the fruits of the Holy Spirit is peace (Gal. 5:22). And if this is one of the fruits of the Holy Spirit, then we ought not to reject peace, or else we are in danger of hell fire (Mark 3:28, 29). Not only this, but if we have the peace of the Holy Spirit, which passes all understanding, and apply it to Psalm 119:165, nothing shall offend us. This may seem like a tall order in a world that we have little to no control over, but that is why we have Jesus Christ Immanuel of Nazareth. He said that He did not come to condemn, but to save (John 3:17). He calls us to forgive (Matt. 18:21-35). And He calls us to be at peace with all men (Rom. 12:18, Heb. 12:14). The reality is that we cannot work to produce this peace; it is a gift from God, like everything else is (Eph. 2:8, 9). So there is no need to be anxious or impatient about receiving this or any other of the fruits of the Holy Spirit, as they come from God freely, in the name of His only begotten Son, Jesus Christ of Nazareth. He died on the cross for the forgiveness of our sins, shedding His Holy and righteous blood at Passover in 31 A.D.. He was buried and the third day, He arose to give us the hope and promise of eternal life in His Holy name. Alleluia and praise the LORD. Amen and Amen.

Discussion Questions

1. What should we do now that we have this information?

   a. God in us
      i. "...greater is he that is in you, than he that is in the world." (1 John 4:4).

2. Who is the ultimate provider of all things? Find some verses in the Bible that confirm your thinking.

   a. Pleasure
      i. Job 36:11
      ii. At the right hand of God (Ps. 16:11).
   b. Food
      i. Psalm 136:25
   c. Shelter
      i. Psalm 23

Printed in the United States
by Baker & Taylor Publisher Services